MAKING FRIENDS
Training Your Dog Positively

Training your dog positively is a good way to make friends with your dog.

MAKING FRIENDS
Training Your Dog Positively

by
Linda Colflesh
Illustrated by Deb Mickey

 **HOWELL BOOK HOUSE**
New York

Collier Macmillan Canada
Toronto

Maxwell Macmillan International
New York   Oxford   Singapore   Sydney

Howell Book House
Macmillan Publishing Company
866 Third Avenue, New York, NY 10022

Collier Macmillan Canada, Inc.
1200 Eglinton Avenue East
Suite 200
Don Mills, Ontario M3C 3N1

Library of Congress Cataloging-in-Publication Data

Colflesh, Linda.
   Making friends: training your dog positively / by Linda Colflesh;
   illustrated by Deb Mickey.
      p.   cm.
   ISBN 0-87605-687-7
   1. Dogs—Training.   1. Title.
SF431.C58   1990   90-4638   CIP
636.7'08'87—dc20

Macmillan books are available at special discounts for bulk purchases for sales promotions, premiums, fund-raising, or educational use. For details contact:

Special Sales Director
Macmillan Publishing Company
866 Third Avenue
New York, NY 10022

10 9 8 7 6 5 4 3 2 1

Printed in the United States of America

To my Mother and Father
To Shauna and Carla, my first dogs
To Brad, my husband

Thank you for the love to grow on.

The author surrounded by some of her friends.

Acknowledgments

THIS BOOK would not have been possible without the support of my husband, Bradford J. Wood, M.D. Brad provided me with a neverending supply of patience and emotional and financial support. In spite of having very limited free time because of his work as a family physician, he gave it up without complaint to take the photographs for the book. He is truly "the wind beneath my wings."

I am grateful to Deb Mickey for her wonderful illustrations. She brings to her illustrations not only her artistic talent, but an understanding of dogs and their owners from her own experiences as an obedience instructor. It was especially nice to be able to work with a good friend who so perfectly shares my own attitudes toward dogs.

A special thank-you must also go to my good friend, Nancy Heckman. She proofread the entire manuscript, and when I needed to talk about my writing, Nancy patiently listened on our many dog walks together. Betsy Keen also gave me important emotional support. Other friends who offered special encouragement are Megan Lloyd and Sally Atwater.

Because I wanted a variety of dogs in the pictures for this book, I had to ask for the help of many friends to pose for them. I want to thank all of them and their cooperative dogs for their time and patience.

Making Friends could not have been written without the help of many friends, both canine and human. Thank you to all of them!

It's best to begin training when your puppy is 9–12 weeks old.

Contents

MAKING FRIENDS
Training Your Dog Positively

The local Humane Society is often the last stop for dogs who don't get trained.   (Siberian Husky)

1

Good Relationships Are Built on Good Training

As A DOG OBEDIENCE INSTRUCTOR, I see many dog owners who are having problems with their dogs. Their dogs won't come when called, drag their owners down the street when walked on leash, jump up on company, chew on furniture, and urinate on the carpets. These owners are frustrated, confused, upset, and sometimes even angry at their dogs. Even though they love each other, they do not understand each other. Both are unhappy.

At least the owners and dogs that I see as an obedience instructor are getting help. As a volunteer worker at an SPCA shelter, I have seen the final ending to many poor dog-owner relationships—death for the dog. Millions of dogs are euthanized every year in the United States. While overpopulation is a part of the problem, many dogs are disposed of by their owners because of behavior problems that could have been solved with good training. I hope through this book to prevent some of these deaths.

I have been teaching dog obedience for thirteen years. I got started by taking my first dog, Shauna, an Irish Setter, to a dog obedience class. We weren't having any problems; it just seemed like a fun thing to do. The obedience training allowed us to do a lot more things together. I could take her to my college classes because she would lie down and stay for fifty minutes. (She had to be very good because dogs weren't supposed to be in the college buildings.) She would ride quietly in the elevator. We could play Frisbee because she would come when called. Best of all, the obedience training helped Shauna and me cope with her timidity, which was the result of poor breeding. When we finished the class, we were awarded a ribbon for being the most improved. At the time I didn't stop to think that being most improved probably meant that we were the worst at the beginning of the class. I was thrilled and decided to pursue an American Kennel Club (AKC) obedience title.

After a lot more work, I showed Shauna in obedience competition. At our second show, we won first place in our class and a big trophy. Now I was really hooked. I continued showing, joined an obedience training club, and was asked to help teach classes. My husband was in medical school and gone a lot of the time, so teaching obedience classes seemed a good way to spend evenings. I discovered that I liked helping people solve their problems with their dogs and was good at it. It was tremendously satisfying to help an owner who came into class threatening to take his dog to the SPCA if things did not improve and left the class pleased with his dog's behavior.

Over the years I continued to learn about dogs and dog training. I learned by experience, by reading everything I could find on dogs, and by attending many dog-training seminars. My best teachers were my dogs. Besides my Irish Setter, I had a Borzoi (also known as a Russian Wolfhound) named Carla. Both are gone now, having died in old age. I learned so much from them. I currently have a Greyhound, and my husband has a Belgian Tervuren that he trained and showed himself. The fact that a busy family physician could put a breed championship, three AKC obedience titles, and a tracking title on his dog tends to discourage arguments from my dog-training students that they don't have time to train their dogs. While we enjoy the challenge of showing our dogs, our primary enjoyment of them is their companionship. I am just as proud of the way they behave at my parents' home when the family gathers for Christmas as I am of any show-ring performance.

I want to help you develop a good relationship with your dog by teaching you to train and understand your dog. My relationships with my dogs over the years have greatly enriched my life. I want to share what I've learned about training dogs so that you, too, can experience the joys of sharing your life with a dog.

GOOD RELATIONSHIPS ARE BUILT
ON REALISTIC EXPECTATIONS

It is regrettable how many times I have had conversations that went something like this:

NEW PUPPY OWNER: My husband and I just found two puppies abandoned by the side of the road. They look like Siberian Huskies. I think they need some training.

ME: Are they housebroken?

NEW PUPPY OWNER: No. They go all over the house.

ME: What have you done to housebreak them?

NEW PUPPY OWNER: Well, nothing really.

ME: Do you have a fenced yard?

NEW PUPPY OWNER: No.

ME: How do you plan to exercise them?

NEW PUPPY OWNER: I guess we'll just train them to stay in the yard.

ME: Do you know how hard it is to train one, let alone *two* Siberian Huskies to stay in an unfenced yard? Siberians are known for their independent natures and urge to run.

NEW PUPPY OWNER: Well, if we can't train them soon, we won't be able to keep them. Will this take more than a few lessons?

What do you think the chances are for these puppies' futures?

Many dog-owner relationships are the victims of unrealistic expectations. Some of these expectations are caused by what we see on television, some are caused by selective memories of childhood dogs, and others are caused by not realizing that all dogs are different.

Dog ownership looks so easy on television. The Lassie myth has been perpetuated by TV shows and dog food commercials. According to TV, you give the dog a little love, throw some dog food at it once a day, and *voilà*—it turns into a completely obedient pet that would gladly give its life to protect its family. My favorites are commercials that show an adorable little child being mobbed by a litter of cute puppies. In reality, puppies of that age are armed with little needles for teeth that send children screaming for their mothers when their arms are punctured. And have you ever seen a dog on TV on leash? No. TV dogs, unlike those in the real world, all immediately come when called. This would all be amusing if the fact of the matter were not that when dogs do not live up to these TV myths, the dog often gets blamed and is disposed of.

People frequently get a dog because a friend or neighbor has one that is wonderful. These people go out and get the same breed, but then are surprised when their dog is different. They are unaware of the great differences in the personalities of dogs of the same breed. Perhaps the neighbor's dog came from a good breeder, while they got theirs from a pet shop. Many of the puppies sold in pet shops are the result of indiscriminate breeding with total disregard for temperament. People also ignore the differences age will make in a dog's behavior, wondering why their eight-month-old Labrador Retriever is a terror, while the eight-year-old Lab down the street is a placid, sweet dog.

I recently was consulted by the owners of a Golden Retriever who could not get over how different the behavior of their dog was from that of the dog's father, who lived down the street. Of course, there was an age difference. Their Golden, Chadley, was just a little more than one year old; his father, Max, was five years old. I explained the behavior differences that this age difference would cause, but they were still doubtful.

One of their major complaints about Chadley was that he jumped up on the kids. The kids didn't like Chadley (which was a reflection of their mother's feelings), but they loved to play with Max. Max never jumped up on them. That's when a little warning bell went off in my head. A Golden Retriever who never jumped up when kids played with him? Either he was an *extremely* well-

Unrealistic expectations often cause dog-owner relationships to fail. One example of this is disappointment over a dog compared to a fondly remembered childhood pet. Even dogs of the same breed can be very different. (Boxer)

Age of a dog, the environment it lives in and the lifestyle of the family it lives with are just some of the factors that will have a bearing on the dog's behavior patterns and how it relates to people and other animals. (Golden Retriever)

trained dog, or, I asked, "Is Max a little overweight?" Bingo! Max was a two-ton tank. He *couldn't* jump up! This "little" difference never occurred to poor Chadley's owners. A little more checking revealed that Max, the supposed saint of dogdom, had stolen a whole chocolate cake from the kitchen counter recently. Max's owners just laughed about it, but when Chadley did the same kind of thing, his owners considered getting rid of him.

People also ignore the differences environment can make in a dog's behavior. The German Shepherd down the street may behave better than yours because his owner is home all day, gives him more exercise, has taken him to obedience training classes, or has a quieter, less stressful household. Dogs today live in a difficult environment. Often both adult members of a household, if there even are two, work outside the home, leaving the dog home all day alone and bored. When I hear an owner complain, "But my old Cocker Spaniel, Buffy, that we had when I was a kid never chewed on the furniture," I remind the owner that Buffy was probably rarely left home alone, could get plenty of exercise running loose around the neighborhood, had other dogs and kids to play with, and was an old dog when they remember her.

Having realistic expectations of your dog will help you anticipate and solve problems. Your dog is a dog and has needs. He needs exercise, company, mental stimulation, and to be taught the rules of the society he lives in. He needs to be forgiven for acting like a dog, even if that is not the way you want him to act.

Is it ever possible to have your own "Lassie"? Yes, with the right dog, the right care, and *the right training*.

CHOOSING A TRAINING METHOD

There are many different ways to train a dog. Of course, you want to choose a method that is easy and effective. However, there should be a more important consideration: the method's effect on your relationship with your dog. A good relationship is based on respect for one another's feelings, so the training method you choose should be one that respects your dog's intelligence and dignity and is as gentle and pleasant as possible.

To help choose a method, try to look at training from your dog's point of view. Imagine that you suddenly find yourself on another planet with beings that don't look or act like you (which is the position your dog is in). You don't understand a word of their language (just like an untrained dog doesn't understand English). You want to fit in somehow and get along with these beings. A being who is significantly bigger than you puts a choke collar around your neck, attaches a leash and pulls on it, giving you the command "Zork." You aren't thrilled about the collar and leash, but you get up and start walking along behind the Big Thing. Suddenly he yells "Zork!" and jerks you forward on the leash. You don't know what you've done wrong, but he seems to want you to walk ahead of him, so that's where you continue walking. This time, he roars "No, Zork!" and gives you a hard jerk backward. Now you're really confused. You don't know where he wants you to walk. After several more painful jerks, you finally figure out that the only place you can walk and not have him jerk you is on his left side. You've learned what "Zork" means, but you're not very anxious to learn more—at least not that way.

Let's try another scenario. You are again helplessly stranded on the planet of Big Things. One of the Big Things comes up to you and shows you that he has a handful of things that look remarkably like candy. He holds one close to your nose so you can sniff it. It smells like candy. You're a little hungry, so when he hands you one, you eat it. Wow, they're great! Big Thing takes a few steps away and says "Zork," all the while holding out the hand with the candy. You take a few steps to follow him, and he hands you another piece. This time when he says "Zork! and walks away, you are quicker to follow him. Again you get another piece. You walk along together, with you respectively a little behind him. He repeats "Zork!" in an inviting tone of voice and lures you forward to his left side with the hand holding the candy. When you get right alongside him, he gives you another piece. You've got it! You get a reward if you walk on his left side when he says "Zork." You can't wait for the next lesson to begin.

The second training example illustrates the use of positive reinforcement. My system of training is based on positive reinforcement, mostly in the form of food rewards. But that isn't the way I've always trained. Everything I read and heard cautioned against using food to train a dog. Then I had a difficult training problem. I wanted to train my Borzoi, Carla, to retrieve. Carla was a beautiful, elegant dog who only did AKC competition obedience to humor me. We had completed her Companion Dog (CD) AKC obedience title. I wanted to try for the next title, the Companion Dog Excellent (CDX), but there was one problem. A dog is required to retrieve to get this title. Carla had never shown any interest in retrieving anything except food from the kitchen counter. I had previously trained my first dog, an Irish Setter, to retrieve reliably for the show ring, but I was uncomfortable with the way I had done it. The method I had used was based on applying force with the choke collar. At the time it was considered a humane method of teaching the retrieve, because the more popular method was to pinch the dog's ear. Nevertheless, it didn't seem the right thing to do morally, causing a dog so much discomfort just to get an AKC obedience title that meant nothing to the dog.

Then I read an article in a dog training magazine about training a dog to retrieve using food. Although I had always been told that you should never use food to train a dog, I was desperate. I decided to try it, and it worked beautifully! Carla got her CDX title easily, and I learned that you *can* train a dog with food.

THE ADVANTAGES OF USING FOOD TO TRAIN YOUR DOG

Training with food is a better way to train dogs. It is easier, more effective, and certainly a lot more fun for you and your dog. Since I trained dogs for many years without using food, I have a good basis for comparison.

6

Training with punishment.

Training with positive reinforcement. Which training method would you prefer?

Training consists of two parts: communicating to your dog what you want, and motivating your dog to do it. Food can help with both. But before you can start, you need to get his attention. Without it, training is impossible. Using food gives you an easy way to get your dog's attention. You have something he wants, so he will be anxious to learn how to get it.

Teaching a dog to lie down is a good example of how food works well for communicating what you want. Say you want to train your full-grown Great Dane, Bruiser, to lie down. You could try to pull him down with the leash. If he decides to resist, and he probably will since it is instinctive for a dog to brace against the force of something pulling on him, you're in for quite a battle. Alternatively, you could lift his front legs when he is sitting and gradually ease him down. Unfortunately, the only thing Bruiser may learn from this is to allow himself to be lifted down, while you get a sore back. Dogs often do not understand that you want them to make a motion on their own, even after you have helped them do that motion many times.

An easier way would be to use food. Attach it to your dog's nose like a magnet, and slowly draw him down to the floor. *Voilà!* Easy, huh? And the motion you make with your hand becomes a hand signal when you no longer need the food in your hand.

The second part of training—motivating your dog to do what you want—involves making a choice. You can make your dog do what you want out of fear of punishment, or you can make your dog work to earn a reward. The use of food to motivate your dog utilizes the psychological principle of positive reinforcement. Positive reinforcement is part of a larger theory of learning known as behavior modification. Basically, the principle of positive reinforcement says that positive reinforcement increases the probability that the behavior preceding it will occur again. For example, if you call your dog and he gets a treat when he comes, he is more likely to come the next time you call. In less fancy terminology, a positive reinforcement is a reward.

While there are many types of rewards for dogs, food is convenient and easy to use, can be given in small amounts, can function as a magnet to draw a dog into a desired position, and is appealing to a wide variety of dogs. It is good for dogs of all ages, from bouncy seven-week-old puppies, to unruly adolescents, set-in-their-ways adult dogs, or fragile old dogs. Food works well for all breeds, from the eager-to-please Golden Retriever to the difficult-to-persuade Chow Chow. It also works for mixed breeds, and for dogs of all personalities. Food is a good tool to build the confidence of shy dogs and to work with aggressive dogs.

Using food as a training tool does not require athletic strength or coordination. It is an ideal method for children, older people, or physically handicapped because of this. And while timing is important in the successful use of food, bad timing of food delivery is not going to cause the problems that bad timing of force causes.

One advantage of training with food is that a child can train a big dog. (German Shepherd)

OTHER REWARDS

There are other rewards in addition to food. A reward, or positive reinforcement, is anything the dog is willing to work to earn. Rewards other than food can be a tennis ball or favorite toy, freedom to explore a new environment, a chasing or wrestling game with the owner, an opportunity to play with other dogs, and praise.

Praise is the only reward utilized in many methods of dog training. In reality praise functions as a very weak reward for most dogs. Trainers who are disdainful of the use of food often assert proudly that their dogs work for praise, implying that their training is superior because their dogs work out of love. However, these trainers are combining praise with strong collar corrections. A good example would be the traditional way of training a dog to heel, which is walking on the handler's left side without pulling on the leash. The dog is commanded to heel, then given jerks on the leash whenever he moves out of the desired position. (Does this sound familiar?) He is then praised when he is back in position. After repetition, the dog responds to the heel command without the leash being jerked, and is praised when he does so. At this point it appears that the dog is working to earn praise. What is really happening is that the dog is working to avoid being jerked on the leash.

Nonetheless, praise is a necessary part of dog training the positive way. Praise strengthens the social bond between dog and trainer. It enables the dog to tell what the trainer is feeling. The dog is accustomed to "reading" his owner's mood by observing his body language and listening to his tone of voice. (Hopefully, you will soon be able to read your dog's body language as well as he reads yours.) The dog needs the reassurance verbal praise provides. The dog is routinely talked to in his daily life with his owner and would be stressed by a sudden silence during training. It's easy to forget to praise your dog when you are also giving food rewards. Actually, you should always praise your dog *before* giving him his food reward. By doing this, the praise takes on the rewarding properties of the food. The praise becomes a "conditioned reinforcer." A conditioned reinforcer is something that is initially meaningless, such as the words "good dog" are to a dog, but through association with an already established reward, the conditioned reinforcer becomes rewarding. Most dogs learn the meaning of "good dog" through unintentional training on the part of the owner. The dog makes an association between the words "good dog" and being petted by a happy owner. With a conditioned reinforcer, you can reward the dog when you don't have food and you can reward behaviors when the dog is away from you and you can't give it food. So praise has two roles: as a conditioned reinforcer, and as reassurance.

You may be worried about your dog's behavior being dependent on the food rewards—that he won't obey your commands unless you have food in your hands. While this is a real concern, I'll show you how to prevent this from happening by using the food properly in training, then gradually reducing your dog's dependence on it.

With a conditioned reinforcer, you can reward the dog when you don't have food and you can reward behaviors when the dog is away from you and you can't give it food. (Great Pyrenees)

THE DISADVANTAGES OF USING FORCE
TO TRAIN YOUR DOG

What happens if you don't use positive reinforcement to train your dog? You'll have to rely more on force, which has many disadvantages. Not the least of these is that people dislike using force on their dogs. It is unfortunate that some dogs never get trained because owners who have been exposed to training based mainly on force and don't like it, ultimately give up on dog training altogether, wrongly assuming that all training is done the same way. Their dogs are then doomed to live in a household where the owner cannot effectively communicate with them. The natural resistance of some dog owners to cause their dogs pain or discomfort is often looked upon by other dog trainers as a lack of character on the part of the new dog trainer. I'll never forget sitting at a seminar for dog obedience instructors and listening to the lecturer saying thankfully, "Trainers become less squeamish as they go along." While using force to train a dog is necessary at times, no one should be forced to lose their inhibitions against causing their dog discomfort.

A major disadvantage of force is that it does not tell a dog what to do, only what *not* to do. A classic example of this problem is seen when people attempt to housebreak a dog by using punishment. The dog is punished whenever it relieves itself in the house. Sometimes what the dog figures out is that in order to avoid punishment, he should be careful not to relieve himself in the presence of his owner. Instead, he will wait until he can get away from his owner to relieve himself in another room or behind the sofa. Taken to extremes, this can result in a dog that will not relieve himself outside when walked on leash because his owner is present. After a lot of suffering, these dogs often end up dead at a Humane Society facility because they supposedly couldn't be housebroken.

Another disadvantage of relying on force to train a dog is that after receiving many small punishments for not performing properly while being trained, the dog reacts by trying to avoid the training situation or even the trainer altogether. Because punishment doesn't let the dog know what the owner wants, the dog may not know how to stop the punishment. When this happens, the dog can develop a sense of helplessness and become depressed or neurotic. Eventually the owner's relationship with his dog may deteriorate to the point where the dog avoids him.

This happens with many dogs that come to me for help after their owners have taken an obedience class in which training is based on force. When the training leash and collar come out, the dog tries to hide or run away. One woman had the frightening experience of having her dog run away in the middle of an obedience class that was being held outdoors under lights after dark. After forty-five terror-filled minutes of searching by driving through fields with her car, she found her dog huddled against a fence, equally frightened.

A dog with a more assertive personality may bite to stop the punishment. One student in a class of mine had that happen to him when trying to teach his German Shepherd, Kahn, to stand on command. I saw Jim giving Kahn a com-

Relying on force to train a dog can make a dog want to avoid training.

mand to stand, but pulling upward on the collar, which was the signal to sit. Kahn, a handsome dog of good temperament, was confused and didn't stand. I explained to Jim what he was doing, but he ignored me. While I was busy with someone else, Jim lost his temper and got rough with Kahn because he was not standing. After a warning growl, Kahn bit Jim—not hard enough to break the skin, but enough to get his point across.

Another disadvantage of force is that often the dog only obeys when on leash. If a dog is trained to obey in order to avoid being jerked on the leash, once the leash is removed the dog's motivation to perform is gone, and so is his training.

A skillful trainer with the right dog may be able to use force without incurring the disadvantages we have just discussed. However, beginner trainers are not skillful, and we don't all have the dogs with the right temperaments for this kind of training. Since there is an easier, kinder way to train a dog, why not use it?

THE ROLE OF FORCE IN POSITIVE TRAINING

In spite of its disadvantages, force may sometimes be necessary when training your dog. Force can be as gentle as lightly restraining a nine-week-old puppy with your hands to teach him to stay. In fact, you are using a very mild form of force whenever you restrain your dog on a leash in order to keep him with you during training. Looking at it this way, force is an unavoidable part of training. In training the positive way you will minimize the use of force, but you will have to use it sometimes. Used in the context of training based on positive reinforcement, the negative effects of force are for the most part counteracted.

Force, when applied to dog training, can mean many different things. As I have already mentioned, it can be restraint. It is more often used as punishment. Force can be either physical or verbal, or a combination of both. Physical force can be in the form of shaking a dog by the collar or scruff of the neck, hitting, spraying the dog with a squirt gun, or making threatening eye contact. However, the most common form of force used in dog training is a jerk of the collar, usually a choke collar. This is often called a "correction," but it is still a form of punishment.

The amount of force you'll have to use depends on many factors, such as the individual personality of your dog, your dog's age when you are starting training, and what you want to accomplish. For instance, a submissive dog of quiet temperament that rarely leaves her quiet house and fenced backyard and started training at twelve weeks of age will need a minimum of force in her training. On the other hand, a large, rambunctious male dog that is just starting training at a year of age, doesn't get enough exercise, and has to be walked on leash in a busy neighborhood will probably need more force.

The situations in which force is useful often involve distractions. If something attracts a dog more than the food, praise, or play you can offer, your dog

A major disadvantage of force is that it does not tell a dog what to do, only what *not* to do. (Great Dane)

There are times in the course of training when the use of force is needed, but the amount of force will vary with the dog, the situation and the needs of the particular moment. (Silky Terrier)

will be distracted. If playing outside on a nice day is more attractive to your dog than the treat he'll get when he comes inside, he won't come in when you call him unless you force him to. If your compulsively friendly Golden Retriever wants to jump on your elderly aunt more than he wants to earn a reward by sitting, forcing him not to jump up is definitely a good idea. However, force should be used only *after* the dog has been trained and you are 100 percent sure he understands what you want.

The use of force in training should not be confused with anger. Trust is an important part of a good relationship with a dog. The fastest way to lose a dog's trust is to let anger get in the way of good training. Anger is usually the result of wrongly blaming your dog for something you dislike or having unrealistic expectations.

To build a good relationship, you have to stop blaming your dog for acting like a dog—for jumping up to greet people, for running away to chase a squirrel, or for relieving his anxiety when he is left home alone by destructive chewing. Destructive behavior while an owner is away is the circumstance that probably triggers the most anger in dog owners. Any group of dog owners can exchange stories of havoc wreaked in their absence: couches chewed to a pulp, irreplaceable molding around windows destroyed, wall-to-wall diarrhea. The list is endless. One of the most memorable I've experienced with my own dogs was returning home to find that our young Belgian Tervuren, Sabre, had pulled a *large* plant out of its pot and then played in the dirt—on our white carpet!

Did we punish him? No! Punishing Sabre would have accomplished nothing other than providing an outlet for our frustration. I'm sure he saw no difference between our indoor plant and the sticks he played with outside. There is no way he could have understood that we were punishing him for something he probably did hours before, so it would have not prevented a future occurrence. I'm sure that if we had yelled at him and acted angry, Sabre would have acted afraid of us. Many people mistakenly interpret this fearful, submissive behavior as the dog knowing he has done wrong, but that's not the case. The point of training is definitely not to make your dog afraid of you. We simply cleaned the mess up and made use of the lesson it taught us, which was that Sabre was not ready to be allowed free run of the house.

Actually, it feels good to be free of getting angry at your dog. Anger gets in the way of loving your dog, and it certainly gets in the way of thinking clearly in order to do good training. You have to learn to be tolerant of your new friend. His values are not the same as yours. He does not value the integrity of your personal possessions, so forgive his mistakes until you teach him not to be destructive. Stop blaming, and start training.

THE MAGIC OF TRAINING THE POSITIVE WAY

The magic of training with positive reinforcement and living with your dog in a positive way is the special relationship you develop with your dog. The

Training should be a way of making friends with your dog. (Golden Retriever)

communication is two-way, rather than the one-way communication of traditional force training. It is always exciting for me to watch a puppy that is just starting training discover this two-way communication. It can happen in a puppy as young as nine weeks. I start by using a treat to teach the puppy to sit. After a couple of repetitions, the puppy figures out that he can make you give him food by sitting in front of you. He starts to follow you around the room, sitting in front of you, without any command or signal from you. I keep rewarding the puppy with a treat. I want him to know he can get my attention by sitting, as opposed to jumping up or barking. But what I really want him to know is that he can communicate with me; I am ''listening'' to him.

When your training is not based on force, your dog is not inhibited from trying new behaviors out of fear of being punished. Your dog thus becomes a much more interesting companion. He shows you more of himself and his intelligence. You learn more about your dog.

Training the positive way makes you and your dog equal partners in the training. Both of you get something you want. You get the good behavior you want, and your dog gets something he wants, as when a puppy exchanges a sit for a treat. The idea of training the positive way is not to dominate a subordinate species, but to communicate with an equal but different one.

Training should be a way of making friends with your dog. Making friends means establishing mutual understanding based on two-way communication, mutual respect, and trust. Training in a positive way will help you accomplish that goal. So let's get started!

2

Housebreaking
the Positive Way

IT IS PROBABLY HARD for you to get excited about developing a good relationship with your dog if he is defecating or urinating in your house. However, since housebreaking is the first training task most dog owners face with a new dog, it often sets the tone for their relationship. Will you start off by creating distrust and fear by punishing him, or will you create trust and understanding by showing your dog in a kind way what it is you want and taking responsibility for helping him do it? Will your dog be a welcome, trusted member of the family who understands the rules, or a pain in the neck who "defies" you, in spite of being hit with a rolled up newspaper, and ruins your carpet by turning it into his bathroom?

Failure to be housebroken may mean a lifetime of being kept outside, isolated from everyone, or it may mean a dog may suffer from being punished constantly for relieving himself indoors. For all too many dogs, failure to be housebroken results in a one-way trip to the local dog pound.

If your dog is already housebroken, you don't need to read this chapter, although you still might find it interesting to glance over. It contains some good examples of using punishment versus positive reinforcement. Skip this chapter only if your dog is *really* housebroken. That means no accidents in the house unless your dog is sick or kept inside longer than he is used to. If you have a male dog, you may want to read the discussion of castration in the section on marking.

Housebreaking the positive way will rely on rewarding your dog for relieving himself where you want him to and on controlling his environment to

Punishment for housebreaking mistakes can cause a dog to hide to relieve himself.

help him form good habits. This method of housebreaking is designed to teach your dog to relieve himself only outdoors. If you live in a large city where you do not have access to a grassy area and have to teach your dog to relieve himself indoors or at a curb of the street, you should refer to a book that teaches this kind of housebreaking.

These techniques apply whether you are trying to housebreak a seven-week-old puppy or an older dog. In some ways it is more difficult to housebreak an older dog because it is hard to change an established habit of relieving himself indoors, but an older dog has the advantage of having better control than a young puppy.

We will not be doing any paper-training. It is not necessary and can be very confusing for a dog when the papers are removed.

PUNISHMENT

Talking about punishment probably seems like a funny way to start a section on housebreaking the positive way. However, punishment is the method many people use to housebreak their dogs, so I want to discuss it right away. Punishment is the cause of a lot of housebreaking problems that can be prevented. You can housebreak your dog without using it at all, which is nicer for both you and your dog and avoids getting your relationship off to a bad start.

All the disadvantages of punishment that were presented in the first chapter apply to housebreaking. The main problem is that it only tells a dog what you don't want, not what you want. Not only does punishment not tell a dog where you want him to relieve himself, but it sometimes isn't even effective at telling a dog where you *don't* want him to go. When punished for relieving themselves in the house, some dogs learn not to relieve themselves in their owner's presence, but to wait until they are gone or to hide and relieve themselves in another room. Once this pattern is established, it is very difficult to break.

This problem can reach incredible extremes. Puff, a three-year-old Bichon Frise, was a typical example of the dogs I see. He had never been housebroken and was brought to me when his owners were moving from their trailer with a linoleum floor to a house with new carpeting. Puff had been punished when he relieved himself in the house, so he had learned to relieve himself only when no one was around. If this meant occasionally waiting for more than twelve hours to find a chance, Puff waited that long.

One of the interesting characteristics that Puff had in common with other dogs who have been punished for accidents is that he wouldn't relieve himself outside. Puff's owners did not have a fenced yard, so they walked him on leash. Unfortunately, Puff had learned the consequences of relieving himself when his owners were present, and since being on leash meant his owners were around, he had decided not to go on leash, either. Puff's owners had kept punishing him for three years in spite of their obvious lack of success because they didn't know what else to do and thus kept reinforcing Puff's ideas. Not only had they not managed to housebreak Puff, they had also created an aggression problem. Puff had started to defend himself from what he perceived to be unreasonable attacks by biting.

Often dogs with this misunderstanding relieve themselves in the least-used room in the house. While it may seem that they have a predilection for oriental carpets, the real reason they are choosing the most expensive carpet in the house is that it is in a room used only for company. This problem also can be confusing if one person in the family is doing most of the punishment, or is punishing more harshly, so the dog acts differently around this person.

Do you recognize some characteristics of your dog in Puff's story? If yes, maybe your dog has received the same wrong message from your punishment. If so, then the first thing you have to do is *stop punishing*. No matter how hard it may be if you see your dog scurrying out of a room as you enter and find he has just relieved himself there, do nothing other than clean it up. To those of you who are just starting housebreaking, learn a lesson from Puff, and don't punish. It does more harm than good.

REWARD

The most important thing to do when housebreaking your dog is to reward him for doing what you want, relieving himself outside. This reward can take the form of praise, but housebreaking will go faster if you use food rewards in addition to praise. It's simple to do. Every time your dog relieves himself outside, give him a treat. What you want is for your dog to rush to relieve himself when you take him outside, then run to you for his treat.

In order to reward your dog for relieving himself outside, you must *always* go outside with him, even if you have a fenced yard. Keep the treats right by the door so you can grab some as you go out. If you want to teach your dog to relieve himself in one particular place in the yard, take him to that place and stay with him until he does. You may want to keep the treats outside by this area in a plastic container. Don't let your dog play until he has relieved himself. You want to establish a habit of him relieving himself before you play, go for walks, or get into the car. You can encourage your dog to use a particular area by placing his feces or the paper towels that you have used to clean up his urine there.

If your dog has been punished and will not relieve himself outside when you are there, you will need to be more patient and do some extra things to get your dog to go outside so you can reward him and communicate what it is you want. Patience may mean staying outside with your dog and waiting for an hour until you can finally reward him. Once he understands what you want, he will get faster and faster at relieving himself.

Some dogs that have had a severe reaction to being punished absolutely refuse to relieve themselves outside on leash. Sometimes they will urinate but not defecate. Dogs have more control over their bowel movements, and often the dog has been caught more frequently in the act of defecating and has consequently been punished for that more often. One easy thing to change is to get a longer leash if the one you are using is only four or six feet in length. Your dog may feel more comfortable if he can get farther away from you. You can make a long leash (twenty to forty feet) out of a piece of rope tied to a bolt snap. This is also a good tool for teaching a dog to come when called and is further described in Chapter 6. If you still cannot get your dog to defecate outside, talk to your veterinarian about using a baby suppository.

CONFINEMENT AND USING A CRATE

Confinement is necessary to prevent accidents when you cannot watch your dog and to encourage him to control his bladder and bowels. Most dogs will instinctively not relieve themselves when confined in a small enough area.

The most effective and safest way to confine your dog is in a crate. A crate is a small cage for dogs. Some dog owners may be upset by the idea of caging their dogs. This is understandable; it seems cruel. However, the fact of the matter is that most dogs, after they get used to their crates, *love* them. They grow attached to them. The crates provide a sense of security. If you watch your dog, you will notice that he naturally chooses places to sleep where he is either under something or his back is up against something. Most dog owners find that even after their dogs are housebroken and no longer need to be crated, they continue to sleep in their crates by choice. I often wonder why my dogs have a special place to go when they want to be left alone and get away from the world, but I don't!

Crates can be made of plastic, which are often the kind used for shipping dogs by air, or of metal wire. Either kind is good for housebreaking. Each has its advantages and disadvantages. The plastic crates are solid and prevent air circulation, which keeps a dog warmer, but may be too warm in hot temperatures. The metal wire crates are often collapsible, which is convenient for taking them with you if you travel with your dog. They provide good air circulation, and can be covered to keep out drafts, if necessary. Some dogs seem to like being able to see out of the metal crates, while others like being hidden in the plastic crates.

Crates can be purchased at pet stores, through the Sears and Penney's catalogues, at dog shows, and through kennel supply catalogues. They also can be rented in some places.

For a crate to work best for housebreaking it needs to be the appropriate size. If it is too big, your dog will be able to eliminate in one end and sleep in the other. The crate should be big enough for him to lie down comfortably, stand up, and turn around, but no larger. It is okay if your dog cannot hold his head up all the way when he is standing or sitting in the crate. For example, a good size crate for a sixty-five pound Golden Retriever is 26″ high, 36″ long, and 24″ wide. A good rule of thumb is to buy a crate that is two to four inches taller than the height of your dog at his shoulders.

These are two different types of crates. The dogs standing beside them show the proper size crate for that dog.   (Belgian Tervuren, Greyhound)

Another means of confinement is an exercise pen.   (English Springer Spaniel)

Buying the right size crate to housebreak a puppy is a more difficult task. The right size crate for an eight-week-old puppy is going to be quickly outgrown. Since some dogs may need to be kept in a crate as adult dogs for reasons other than housebreaking problems, such as destructive behavior when left alone, it is more practical to purchase the size crate your dog will need as an adult. If you do this and find that your puppy is relieving himself in the crate, find a way to block off part of the crate, such as with a piece of plywood. If you think your dog will be spending a lot of time in the crate, you might want to give your dog a little more room to move around by buying one size larger than necessary.

When you get your crate, you will have to choose a place to put it. There are many options. I like keeping mine in my bedroom. In fact, I have made covers for the crates to match my bedspreads! While my dogs are young puppies and I have to use the crates frequently, I move the crates into the kitchen area during the day. The kitchen is a popular place to keep a crate, if your kitchen is large enough. Puppies are often confined to kitchens anyway because of the easy-to-clean floor, and the kitchen is a place where the family spends a lot of time. Other good places to put a crate are in a utility room, the family room, or a room of the house that isn't used often.

You may want to put some sort of bedding in the crate. Obviously, washable bedding is a good idea. Many dogs like the washable, imitation pieces of fleece that are available for dogs. If your dog shows any inclination to chew his bedding, however, you will have to remove it. Swallowing fabric can cause a life-threatening intestinal blockage. My dogs have their own personal preferences regarding bedding in their crates. Our Belgian Tervuren consistently pulls out anything we put in his crate before he goes into it. On the other hand, our Greyhound has little natural padding of her own, so she appreciates as much padding as we can stuff into her crate.

To introduce your puppy or dog to his new crate, set the crate up and allow your dog to examine it. Put treats in the crate, at first near the door, then later toward the back so he has to go all the way in to get them. Avoid forcing your dog into the crate. Throughout the first day or two, drop treats into the back of the crate every few hours. When your dog is walking in and out freely, without any fear, start feeding him in his crate. Up until now, you should not have closed the door, but once he is contentedly eating in his crate, you can close and latch the door while he is eating. Gradually extend the period of time he is shut in.

If at any time your dog starts barking, whining, or pawing at the door of the crate because he wants to be let out, *do not let him out.* Ignore his efforts to get your attention, or tell him ''no'' in a firm tone of voice. Don't let him out until he is quiet and has settled down. You don't want him to learn that he can get you to open the door by carrying on.

Start associating a command with putting your dog in his crate. Take your dog to his crate (dog treat in hand), throw the treat in, then give him the command as he enters the crate. My command is a highly unoriginal ''Get in your crate.'' I have a student who refers to her dog's crate as her ''apartment.''

How long should you keep your dog in his crate? This is a difficult question to answer. A young puppy of seven to twelve weeks of age cannot hold his urine for more than a few hours, so don't crate him longer than that, except at night. Gradually build up to four hours. By twelves weeks of age, your puppy should be able to go eight hours at night while he is sleeping. You should avoid crating your dog for more than four to five hours if at all possible, except at night.

WARNING: *Never put your dog in a crate with a collar on.* He could catch his collar on part of the crate and strangle himself in his struggle to get free. Many dogs have. This is true for any kind of collar. Don't take chances.

There are other ways to confine a dog besides using a crate. One way is to keep your dog on leash and with you wherever you are in the house. You can tie the leash to a piece of furniture while you are in the room, or to your bed at night. Another way is to tie your dog with a short chain (approximately four feet long) to a screw eye fastened into your wall in a place you spend a lot of time, such as the kitchen. However, you should *never* leave your dog alone on such a chain. He could get tangled and choke himself, or he may chew on whatever furniture or baseboard is within reach.

Laundry rooms or bathrooms can work, if the rooms are small enough, aren't carpeted, and your dog won't be destructive. Cover the floor with newspaper at first. Remove anything your dog may get into, like toilet paper, soap, and towels hanging down. Your dog will probably object strenuously if you shut the door to this room while you are home. It is amazing what dog claws can do to a door. If you have to confine him there when you are home, it would be better to block the door with a baby gate. That way your puppy will feel less isolated.

Some people confine their dogs in basements, or back porches or in garages while they are away. However, these places are not small enough to inhibit a dog from relieving himself. Housebreaking to the rest of the house may be more difficult because your dog may have trouble understanding that he can relieve himself in one part of the house but not in the rest.

Some dogs will relieve themselves even though they are confined to a small space. Dogs from pet shops who have been kept confined in small cages where they have no choice but to relieve themselves in their cages loose their normal inhibitions against this. Confinement sometimes doesn't work with them, or it takes longer to work. Also, if a dog is relieving himself inside the crate, even though he has not been left there long, it may be a sign that your dog has a bladder infection. See "Health Problems," page 37, for more information about this.

Other dogs panic at being confined and relieve themselves out of fear. These dogs may adjust given time and careful handling, but some may not. I experienced this kind of problem with my Greyhound, Zephyr. Even though she was seven weeks old when I got her and introduced her to the crate, she took what seemed like forever to adjust to it. In the meantime, I cleaned up several accidents in the crate. I had never had this problem with any of my previous dogs. I think she had problems adjusting because she was a very energetic puppy and tended to be overemotional about everything. She stopped defecating in her crate in a few days, and stopped urinating in it two weeks later. In spite of her poor start, Zephyr loves her crate and now happily runs to it from anywhere in the house whenever I say, "Get in your crate." Of course, the dog biscuit she always gets when I put her in the crate probably helps a lot. If your dog does not adjust to the crate, try some of the other alternatives listed in this chapter.

Please give crate training a chance, even if you have serious misgivings. I had those same feelings when I was first introduced to the idea of a crate. I didn't believe dogs would really love them as much as they do. Many dogs destroyed each year because they couldn't be housebroken or were destructive when left alone could have been saved with crate training.

CONFINEMENT WHEN YOU WORK ALL DAY

Housebreaking and confining your puppy or dog while you are away at work eight or more hours each day presents special problems that demand special solutions. A puppy cannot go eight hours without relieving himself until he is five or six months old. While he is young, or while an older dog is being housebroken, you must confine him in an area large enough to permit him to sleep in a separate area from where he relieves himself, but small enough to encourage him to try to control his eliminations.

A bathroom or utility room will do, as mentioned above, but it has to be larger if your dog is going to be left there for longer hours. Put down newspapers in one part of the room, and something for your dog to lie on in another part. Leave him a small amount of water. My Borzoi was housebroken by being left in a bathroom while I was at work. It was very effective, and throughout her life, Carla loved sleeping in the bathroom, wrapped around the cool base of the toilet or curled up in the bathtub. In fact, we had to tie the bathroom door open when we were gone because oftentimes Carla would stretch out on the cool tile floor and shut the door on herself by mistake.

Another option is to use an exercise pen set up inside. This is a pen without a top or bottom, and it usually folds flat for storage. They are made of eight connecting panels, ranging in height from twenty-four inches to forty-five inches. I recommend putting a sheet of plastic underneath, and then covering the area with newspapers.

If you confine your dog in the kitchen, I would suggest blocking off part of the room. Most kitchens are too big for effective housebreaking. With a little ingenuity, you can build a barrier, perhaps with a hinged gate to allow easy access.

You can still use a crate to housebreak your dog, but arrangements need to be made to let your dog out halfway through the day. If you cannot arrange to come home from work over your lunch hour during the few weeks or months it may take to housebreak your dog, perhaps you can persuade a neighbor, relative, or friend to drop by and let your dog out. Offer an exchange for their help. Perhaps you could take care of their pet when they are away on a weekend. You could also hire someone to come in and let your dog out to relieve himself.

Some people leave their dogs outdoors in a kennel or fenced yard while they are away at work. Unfortunately, this is often not safe for your dog. First of all, dogs are stolen out of such enclosures. If you are using a fenced yard, your dog could learn to climb the fence while you are gone. Your dog is helplessly exposed to the teasing of neighborhood children, and this can lead to an aggression problem. Your dog may develop a barking problem that annoys your neighbors. The safest place to leave your dog is inside your house.

When you are home, continue to restrict your dog's freedom and supervise him closely to prevent accidents. Pick up any soiled newspapers as soon as you get home, and do not put down fresh ones until you are ready to leave the next morning. The papers are only being used to protect your floor, not to paper-train your dog. Don't let your dog use them when you are home. If, while you are home, your dog tries to relieve himself where he is kept during the day, block off that room or area.

GIVING YOUR DOG MORE FREEDOM

One of the most common mistakes people make when housebreaking their dogs is giving their dog too much freedom too soon. If your seven- to twelve-week-old puppy is having more than one accident every three days, you are giving him too much freedom. The same holds true for a three- to five-month-old puppy that is having more than one accident a week, and for a dog over five months old that is having any accidents.

A good time to give your dog more freedom is right after you have taken him out and seen him relieve himself. If he is in the seven- to twelve-week age range, limit this to fifteen minutes to half an hour, and keep him in one room. When he looks like he is about to take a nap, put him back in his crate and shut the door. Gradually give him more time out of the crate and access to more rooms, one room at a time. The use of expandable baby gates is invaluable. They come extra-tall and extra-wide, and can even be double stacked if your dog is a good climber or jumper. If your dog has an accident, you've given him too much freedom and need to cut back.

There can be a problem with confining your dog too much. For example, a puppy kept exclusively in a kitchen until he is six months old may not regard the rest of the house as part of his home that he instinctively wants to keep clean. While your puppy is young, or while you are in the process of housebreaking an adult dog, it is wise to give them brief, supervised access to whatever rooms in the house the dog will be allowed in when he is housebroken.

You will also want to try giving your dog more freedom when you are away from home. Again, start with one room. Try it when you are going out for a short errand. Slowly extend the time you leave your dog alone, and add more rooms.

Do not assume that because your dog is housebroken in your house, he will not eliminate in other people's homes. Even if he is perfect at home, restrict his

A sample housebreaking diary.

freedom in other people's homes by keeping him on leash until you are sure you can trust him. It is best to avoid mortifying experiences, like the time our young male dog lifted his leg on my sister-in-law's Christmas tree!

SCHEDULING

It is easiest to housebreak your dog if you keep him on a schedule. He will know when to expect to be taken out to relieve himself, and you will learn when he needs to go.

Start by feeding your dog on a schedule. Pick convenient times, with the number of meals dependent on the age of your puppy, and stick with these times, even on weekends. Do not leave food available during the day. If your dog doesn't finish what you put down, pick it up and either save it or throw it away.

If you feed your dog at the same times every day, he should have to defecate at corresponding times. You'll be able to predict when these times are. To learn what your dog's schedule is, keep a housebreaking diary. Write down for five days what time you feed your dog, how much he eats (more about amounts of food later), when he defecates, when he urinates, where he eliminates (in the house or outside!), and what he was doing right before he urinated. You will need to get all the members of your family to cooperate.

Soon you should begin to see a pattern. Your dog should defecate at approximately the same times each day. If these times are not convenient for you, gradually change his feeding times. When your dog urinates is probably more related to what he is doing than what time it is. Dogs usually have to urinate when they first wake up in the morning and when they wake up from any naps during the day. Puppies are especially susceptible to lack of bladder control when they get excited and are playing.

Your housebreaking diary will identify the times when your puppy or dog has accidents in the house. Use this information to figure out what you are doing wrong and what you can do to solve it. Perhaps at certain times of the day you are too busy, and your dog is not being supervised adequately. Is it when the kids get home from school, or when you are fixing dinner? Whenever these times occur, you may want to confine your dog. Are the accidents occurring in one place in the house? Maybe you are not completely getting the smell of the urine or stool out of the carpet, and so the smell is attracting your dog back to the same place. Is your dog only having accidents in rooms when you aren't there? Your dog may be confused by your punishment.

FEEDING

As discussed above, feeding your dog on a schedule will make housebreaking easier. How much and what you feed your dog will also have an effect.

It helps if you feed your dog a high-quality dry dog food. The better quality

Overfeeding can make housebreaking difficult, not to mention a fat dog.

dog foods have less filler in them, thereby producing a smaller volume of feces, less frequent bowel movements, and firm stools. Dry dog food is best because it is more economical than canned dog food, is better for your dog's teeth, and does not contain the chemicals and sugars of the semimoist, burger-type dog foods. Many people are not aware that most of the premium-quality dry dog foods are not sold in supermarkets. These foods cost more but usually are fed in smaller quantities. They are available in pet stores and at some kennels. If you are having a housebreaking problem with defecating in the house, it is worth trying one of these foods.

Like people, all dogs react differently to different foods. What agrees with your neighbor's dog may cause diarrhea in yours. Also, if you keep switching foods, your dog's intestines will have to keep readjusting and he may have intermittent diarrhea from this. Once you have found a dog food that is good for your dog, stick to it. Feed the same amount of the same food every day, keeping in mind your dog's changing nutritional needs as he matures. Don't add table scraps, and don't give between-meal treats except as necessary for training. These rules may be relaxed when your dog is completely housebroken, but not until then. It is hard enough for your dog to control his bowels when you are gone for long periods of time. Don't make it harder on him by feeding him improperly.

Another feeding problem that interferes with housebreaking is feeding your dog too much. It is hard to tell what amount to feed a dog, especially a growing puppy. This is complicated by the fact that the amounts suggested on the bag of dog food are too much for most dogs. Overfeeding can cause frequent bowel movements and stools of soft consistency, which makes it harder for your dog to control his bowels. It can even cause diarrhea. One way to tell if you are overfeeding your dog is the consistency of his stools, which should be firm. If your dog is not finishing the food you give him, he is probably being overfed. While fat, roly-poly puppies may be appealing, it is better for your dog's health to keep him on the slim side. Overfeeding has been shown to exacerbate some diseases, such as hip dysplasia.

CLEANING UP

It is important that any accidents your dog has in your house be thoroughly cleaned up. If there is any remaining scent, the smell will attract your dog to relieve himself in that area again.

The thing *not* to use to clean up urine or feces is an ammonia-based product. Urine contains ammonia, so you are just adding more if you use such a product. The lingering ammonia smell may attract your dog back to the place you just cleaned up.

The best cleaning products are those specially designed for this purpose. They are available in pet stores or sometimes at veterinarians. Bacteria/enzyme products work best. Look for this on the label. If you are doing a good job with housebreaking and accidents are kept to a minimum, it may not be necessary to purchase such a product. Instead you can use a mixture of half water and half white distilled vinegar. This is convenient to use if kept in a spray bottle.

Whatever you use, blot up the urine well. Do it as soon as possible to prevent the urine from spreading deeper into the carpet. Remove as much moisture as possible. Then follow the directions on the pet stain cleaning product or spray with the vinegar-water mixture. Blot some more, then place a thick stack of paper towels on the spot and weigh it down with a heavy book. Put aluminum foil or plastic wrap between the book and towels to protect the book.

ASKING TO GO OUT

Many dog owners are concerned because their dogs don't ask to go out. Many dogs do not, and this is not necessary to housebreak a dog. You should be taking your dog out on a regular enough basis and frequently enough that he doesn't have to ask to go out.

Some dogs learn to ask to go out on their own, without being taught. These are usually dogs with more assertive personalities. A passive dog may never ask to go out, or he may give hard-to-read signs, such as pacing, whining, or just looking uncomfortable.

I have one dog that asks to go out, and one that does not. Zephyr asks to go out by standing at the back door, hitting the doorknob with her nose, and whining. She learned to do this on her own. Our older dog, Sabre, never asks to go out. Interestingly, if Sabre is sick and needs to go out right away, he attempts to communicate this to us by staring at us. If he is desperate, he will wake us up at night or stand by the back door. So even though he does know how to ask to go out, he chooses not to do so normally. And Sabre has *never* had an accident in the house since he was a puppy.

There are, in fact, disadvantages to having a dog learn to ask to go out. Some dogs will start asking to go out whenever they want their owner's attention, or just to play outside. It is hard to tell if the dog has to relieve himself or not.

If you think it would be helpful in your situation, you can teach your dog to ask to go out. Before you take him out the door, take his paw and hit it against the door. Another option is to tie bells to the doorknob for your dog to ring. Hang the bells so they are on the dog's level. You can also use a set of the sleigh bells people hang on their doorknobs during the Christmas season. Hit the bells with your dog's paw before you go out. Once your dog is housebroken, you can take the bells down if your dog is ringing them constantly for attention.

REALISTIC EXPECTATIONS

I want to give you some idea of what you can realistically expect when housebreaking your dog. How fast this program can work depends on many

This dog is hitting bells to indicate he wants to go outside. (Shetland Sheepdog)

factors. An excitable puppy will take longer than a laid-back one. Housebreaking in a busy household in which chaos rules is harder than in a quiet one on a regular schedule. And an older dog with a well-established habit of relieving himself inside will take longer than a puppy or an older dog that has been previously kept outside.

If you start with a seven- to twelve-week-old puppy and follow the above program religiously, you may be able to limit the number of accidents in your house to two or three. However, if your puppy is under four months old, it is to be expected that he will often lose control of his bladder when he gets excited. If you are following this program and after three weeks are having more than one accident a week, you are probably doing something wrong. Check the trouble-shooting list at the end of this chapter, and reread the chapter.

Your dog should be completely housebroken by the time he is six months old. By *completely housebroken* I mean able to be taken with complete confidence to visit your mother-in-law who is not very fond of dogs and has expensive oriental carpets.

If you feel your dog is not progressing fast enough in his housebreaking, seek the help of a professional dog trainer who counsels clients about this problem. The longer your dog continues to relieve himself in the house, the harder it will be to housebreak him. Don't wait too long!

SUBMISSIVE URINATION

Some dogs lose control of their bladders when they greet people, either family members or strangers. This is different from other housebreaking problems. It is called *submissive urination* by dog behaviorists. It is a normal canine greeting behavior. A dog that does this has no conscious control over his urination at the time. This is a common behavior in puppies, and usually goes away as they mature. Some dogs are as old as two years before they stop submissively urinating. Rarely it may persist in some dogs throughout their lives. Submissive urination can be a difficult problem to solve, but there are some things you can do to help.

First of all, because your dog has no conscious control over it, punishment will certainly not help. In fact, it will make things worse because the punishment will increase his submissive behavior. Even a slightly raised voice to a dog with this problem will cause him to urinate submissively. The best thing to do when this happens is to simply ignore it and clean it up.

If your dog urinates in excitement when you arrive home, make your arrival as calm and matter-of-fact as possible. When you get home, try not to talk to him for the first five minutes. Of course, try to greet your dog outside to eliminate cleanup. You might also try distracting your dog with a treat or by throwing a ball if he is a compulsive retriever.

The best thing you can do for this problem is to build your dog's confidence. Take him to different places and let him meet as many people as possible.

Attending an obedience training class is a great way to do this. Your dog will get exposure to a different place and to people and other dogs. Bring a roll of paper towels to the first few classes in case of accidents.

MARKING

If you have a male dog who is lifting his leg on your furniture, your housebreaking problem may be hormonally related. The best solution is castration, which removes the source of the hormones that cause this housebreaking problem. The sex-related hormones that are released in a male dog as he sexually matures cause your dog to have urges to mark his territory by urinating on upright objects. While castration is not a 100 percent cure, it works well most of the time, combined with other housebreaking techniques. This does not mean it is impossible to housebreak an intact male. However, if you have this problem, housebreaking will be much easier if your dog is castrated.

The strength of the urge to mark varies in male dogs. In some, the urge seems to be so strong that it is almost beyond their conscious control. These dogs are often described by their owners as "high-strung" or "hyper." They are sometimes hard to keep weight on. Castration helps all these problems. Some dogs become housebroken within days after surgery, after many months of marking problems.

Castration is an emotionally charged subject for many dog owners. It is perfectly understandable that people feel uncomfortable about surgically removing part of their dog's anatomy. Many people are afraid of how their dog might change. Still others are attracted to the idea of using their dog at stud. However, dogs only change for the better following castration. Dogs who protect the house continue to do so; hunting dogs work just as well after as before. Some dogs gain weight following castration. They simply need to have the amount of food they eat reduced. If the weight gain doesn't respond to a change in diet, you might want to have your veterinarian run a thyroid test on your dog, which requires analysis of a blood sample.

People often want to have their male dog sire a litter of puppies because they love their male dogs and want to see their good qualities reproduced. Making money and satisfying a male dog's sexual urges are other reasons people want to use their dogs at stud, even though these are poor reasons. Unfortunately, there are millions of unwanted dogs killed every year. The world doesn't need more dogs. Only the very best male dogs should be used at stud—those that have been screened by experts for the genetic problems that plague dogs, have had their pedigrees examined by someone knowledgeable, and have been judged by someone both knowledgeable and objective (not the owner or breeder of the dog) to be outstanding specimens of their breed. Realistically, the chances are slim that an owner of a quality female dog will want to use your dog at stud.

It is kinder to castrate your dog than to subject him to a lifetime of being punished, even if it's just verbally, for urinating in the house. Uncastrated male dogs are not genetically cut out to live in the world they find themselves in as our pets and are often cruelly frustrated. Castration is a simple, safe surgical procedure that will reduce your dog's cancer risks and the chance of prostate problems, as well as make his life more comfortable emotionally.

HEALTH PROBLEMS

If you are having problems housebreaking your dog, it is imperative that you make sure he does not have a health problem. The most common is a bladder infection. Male or female dogs can have this problem, and the symptoms are easy to overlook. Bladder infections are more common in young puppies whose immune systems are not mature enough to combat infections. And don't be fooled by the fact that your puppy has had a veterinary examination when he got his shots. The veterinarian cannot tell if your puppy has a bladder infection by an examination. The only way to check is with a urine sample. You can collect this sample at home and take it in while it is still fresh, or refrigerate it until you can get it to the veterinarian. Of course, collecting the sample may provide any nosy neighbors with a lot of entertainment.

One of the symptoms of a bladder infection is frequent urination of small amounts. A dog with a bladder infection will often relieve himself in his crate. If you suspect your puppy is relieving himself more often than normal, you would be wise to have a urine sample checked. Treatment is usually by antibiotics.

There are other causes for lack of bladder control, such as an obstructed bladder, an enlarged prostate gland, or kidney failure. Older female dogs who have been spayed sometimes start to lose control over their bladder because they have a deficiency of estrogen, a hormone that is important in maintaining the bladder tone. This can be treated by a veterinarian. Frequent urination and lack of bladder control can be a side effect of cortisone, a drug used often in veterinary medicine.

I'll never forget the story of Buttons, a cute, shaggy three-year-old mixed breed who signed up for one of my obedience classes. Buttons just didn't seem healthy. There was something about the look in her eyes, and she lacked the stamina to work for the whole hour of the class. I expressed my concern to her owner and asked about Buttons' health, including if she was having frequent urination or housebreaking problems. She said no, although questioning did reveal that Buttons had been on cortisone for flea-allergy problems for many months. Repeated questioning over the next few weeks finally elicited the information that Buttons was paper-trained because she could not hold her urine for very long. Her owner had never had another dog and assumed that this was normal! I quickly sent her off to her veterinarian and, sure enough, Buttons had a bladder infection. Who knows how long she had had it, since the veterinarian had noted a slightly elevated temperature on her last exam a year previously! It could have been that the immunosuppressive nature of the cortisone made But-

Getting a urine sample can be awkward, but it is a necessary procedure if you suspect a bladder infection. (German Shorthaired Pointer)

Buttons. (Mixed breed)

tons at increased risk for getting a bladder infection. In any case, after ten days of treatment with antibiotics and elimination of the cortisone, Buttons' owner picked up the newspapers and never had to use them again. In addition, her "couch potato" dog was full of new energy, able to play and participate in the family activities.

Another health problem that interferes with housebreaking is diarrhea. There are many causes of diarrhea, some that can be frustrating to diagnose and cure. The effect of overfeeding on stool volume and consistency has already been discussed. Among the causes of diarrhea are worms, protozoan infections, food intolerance, pancreatic enzyme deficiency, and viruses. Some of these are difficult to diagnose, so you and your veterinarian must be persistent in searching for a cause and the right treatment.

TROUBLESHOOTING CHECKLIST

Still having trouble with accidents in the house? Maybe you've missed something in this chapter. Go over this checklist carefully, and see if there is something you are not doing.

_____ 1. Are you keeping your dog confined when you cannot watch him, even if you are in the house with him?

_____ 2. Did you keep a housebreaking diary for five days?

_____ 3. Are you careful to feed your dog at the same time every day? Measuring his food? Not overfeeding? No snacks? No table scraps? Not switching foods?

_____ 4. Is everyone in your family cooperating in your housebreaking efforts?

_____ 5. Are you punishing your dog and confusing him?

_____ 6. Are you sure your dog isn't sick and needs to be checked by a veterinarian?

_____ 7. Do you always go outside with your dog so that you know whether he has relieved himself and so you are able to reward him?

_____ 8. Are you completely getting the scent of your dog's urine and/or stools out of the carpet?

_____ 9. Are you giving your dog too much freedom in the house?

_____ 10. Are you expecting too much self-control from a young puppy?

Housebreaking works best when combined with obedience training that helps you and your dog understand each other better, so let's move on.

Don't be misled. AKC papers are not a guarantee of quality.

3

Getting Off
to a Good Start

IT IS MUCH EASIER to train a dog and your chances of success are much greater if you get off to a good start. Ideally, this means starting when you bring your puppy home, at between seven and twelve weeks of age. If you have a puppy between those ages, this chapter is for you.

Many of you reading this book probably already have a dog older than twelve weeks. Unfortunately, some people don't seek training information until after they have gotten off to a *bad* start and are having trouble with their dog. Even if your dog is older than twelves weeks, you should read this chapter. You can compare the positive training method with how your dog was handled in his first twelve weeks, or, if you don't know, how you guess he was handled, and that will help you understand your dog now. You'll be more patient when training your older dog if you understand that he lacked the advantages of being trained at an early age.

Whether you are starting with a puppy, with an older dog you've just adopted, or trying to build a new relationship with a dog you've had for a while, you will begin by teaching commands in the way described under ''Teaching Commands: Sit, Stay, Okay, and No.'' No matter what your dog's age, he needs to have his confidence built up through socialization; this process is discussed in ''Building Confidence.'' The principles presented in ''Street Training'' can be applied to an older dog, although the results of the training will be less dependable.

The first section is about choosing a dog. Discovering the mistakes you made in choosing your dog may help prevent you from blaming him for not being what you expected. You will be better prepared next time you get a dog. You could even pass this information along to a friend who is getting a dog!

CHOOSING A DOG

Getting off to a good start begins with choosing the right dog. Remember the discussion about realistic expectations in the first chapter? I said it was possible to have your own "Lassie" if you use the right care, the right training, and the right dog. Getting the right dog is an important part of this equation. Part of the Lassie myth that leads people to have unrealistic expectations is the belief that dogs are basically all alike and, with enough love, any dog can become a great pet. Unfortunately, this just isn't true. Some dogs are born with bad temperaments that no amount of love and training can fix or health problems that will run up expensive veterinary bills.

Selecting a good dog is a process full of pitfalls. However, you can maximize your chances of getting the perfect dog for you by making well-informed choices. If you already have a dog, compare this information with how you chose him. It may help you understand your dog better.

Among your first choices are pure-bred versus mixed breed, puppy versus older dog, and whether to rescue a dog from a Humane Society shelter or go to a breeder. These decisions depend partially on your personal preferences, but try to be aware of the problems you can run into. Because of the genetic problems associated with many pure-bred dogs, your odds of getting a healthy dog of good temperament are probably better by selecting a mixed breed instead of a pure-bred dog that is the result of a random, indiscriminate breeding. However, getting a mixed breed is not an automatic guarantee of health or good temperament.

If you decide to purchase a pure-bred dog, you must be careful. In order to maintain the uniformity of appearance of pure-bred dogs, the gene pool is limited. This makes it more likely that the genes responsible for health and temperament problems will surface. There are at least 150 defects strongly suspected to be genetic in dogs. Because of this, pure-bred dogs must be very carefully bred. To get a good pure-bred dog, you must avoid litters that are the result of indiscriminate breeding—breedings that are done without regard for the quality of the dogs involved.

It is easy to be deceived about the quality of a pure-bred dog. This deception is often unintentional on the part of the breeders, who may themselves be uninformed about the quality of the dogs they are breeding. Buyers of pure-bred dogs often wrongly interpret statements such as these:

"These dogs are AKC registered." AKC registration has nothing to do with the quality of a dog. The American Kennel Club does not screen dogs for good temperament or absence of hereditary health problems before they register them. The only thing AKC registration means is that the puppy was the result of a mating of two registered dogs. Even that isn't guaranteed, as it is easy to obtain registration papers under false pretenses.

"These dogs are from champion lines." Puppy buyers are often impressed by seeing a champion or two on a pedigree, even though these champions are

several generations removed from the puppy they are considering purchasing. Unfortunately, any influence these champions may have had on the quality of a dog can be negated by one indiscriminate breeding. If these champions are not your puppy's sire or dam, don't be mistakenly impressed by them. An AKC championship is not an absolute guarantee of quality anyway. It is possible to show a dog with hip dysplasia, a hereditary disease that affects a dog's hip joint, to a championship.

"My dogs have never had any trouble with hip dysplasia." Some puppy buyers have done enough research on the breed they are purchasing to know that the breed has hereditary problems, such as hip dysplasia. When they ask about it, the above statement may be the answer they receive. The only way hip dysplasia can be reliably diagnosed is with an X ray of the sire and dam prior to breeding. These X rays are then often submitted to the Orthopedic Foundation for Animals (OFA) to be evaluated by veterinary radiologists. If the X ray shows good hip joints, the dog is then given an OFA number. This number is not given to dogs under two years of age, because not all cases can be detected until then. If you hear this line, ask if the dogs have been x-rayed.

"This dog is from a kennel (or breeder), not a pet shop." Some people know enough to avoid the high-priced and often low-quality puppies available at pet shops, but are unable to distinguish between good and bad breeders and kennels. Anyone who owns a female dog and breeds it is a breeder, but not necessarily a good one! Even more confusing is the term *kennel*. It can refer to a breeder of show dogs who keeps her two dogs in the house and raises one litter every two years in her family room. It can also refer to someone who mass produces puppies of several breeds without regard to quality using dogs who spend their entire lives in cages.

"This puppy comes with a guarantee." Read the fine print. Many guarantees require that you return the original puppy before you will be given a replacement. However, you will already be in love with your first puppy and unwilling to give it up, especially to an uncertain fate. And would you want another puppy from a breeder who has already been proven to produce problem dogs? Your best guarantee is careful shopping before you buy a dog.

These are just some examples of ways to be misled when purchasing a dog. Let them serve as warnings: Be careful!

If you are getting an older dog, beware of hidden problems. People often give up an older dog because of a behavior problem, one they may not be honest about in order to place the dog in a new home. If possible, you may want to arrange for at least a one-week and preferably a one-month trial period, during which time you can return the dog if you run into a problem.

Where should you look for a good puppy? The best litters are often never advertised in newspapers. Your local kennel club may be able to refer you to a good breeder, but it may not be listed in the phone book. A veterinarian, groomer, or boarding kennel may be able to put you in touch with the local kennel club. If not, addresses can be obtained from the American Kennel Club, 51 Madison Ave, New York, NY 10010. You can also obtain from the AKC the address of the national breed club for the AKC-registered breed you are interested in. This breed club should be able to refer you to the breeders closest to you.

Don't be afraid of dealing with breeders who competitively show their dogs, even though you only want a good pet. People who go to the trouble of showing their dogs generally give a lot of thought to how they breed them. Few breedings of show dogs produce a litter of strictly show-quality puppies. The puppies that cannot be successfully shown because of minor cosmetic faults are also the product of this careful breeding and will be placed in homes as pets. Show dogs are rarely successful unless they have stable temperaments and are able to withstand the stress of shows. They have to allow a stranger, the judge, to approach them and to stand still while the judge runs his hands over their bodies. Stable temperaments, low susceptibility to stress, and tolerance of strangers handling them are all good traits in a pet.

CHARACTERISTICS OF A GOOD BREEDER

Some things to look for in locating a conscientious dog breeder:

1. A good breeder only breeds one or two breeds, as it is difficult to be truly knowledgeable about more breeds than that.
2. A good breeder will not be anxious to sell you a dog until he or she questions you closely to see if you will be a good dog owner.
3. A good breeder will raise his puppies so that they have a lot of contact with people. The puppies will be in a clean environment.
4. A good breeder will be able to tell you the genetic problems within his particular breed and what he has done to reduce the chances of these problems occurring in the dogs he is producing.
5. A good breeder will be knowledgeable about the breed standard set by the breed's national organization and how well his dogs meet this standard.
6. A good breeder can tell you why the breeding partners were selected and what characteristics they will hopefully produce. He will also be knowledgeable about genetics and be able to tell you if the puppies are the product of inbreeding, line breeding, or an outcross, all methods that can produce good puppies in the hands of a good breeder.
7. A good breeder does not sell puppies to a pet shop or another third party because he or she wants to have control over the homes the puppies are placed in.
8. A good breeder sells pet-quality puppies with spay-neuter agreements.
9. A good breeder breeds infrequently, usually no more than two litters a year, and often as infrequently as one litter every two years.
10. A good breeder provides complete instructions on feeding, veterinary care, etc., with each puppy, as well as a written guarantee and contract. He is anxious to educate the buyers of his puppies.

11. Good breeders are committed to the welfare of the breed as well as their individual dogs.
12. A good breeder will want to be informed if at any time you can no longer keep your dog.
13. A good breeder will show his dogs, as this is the best way of obtaining an objective opinion regarding how well a dog measures up to the breed standard.

Once you have decided on a breeder and a litter, you will be faced with the task of selecting a puppy from the litter. The best age to get a dog is between seven and twelve weeks of age, with closer to seven weeks being preferable. At seven weeks of age, puppies have been with their littermates long enough to have had the experiences necessary for them to develop normally, yet they are young enough to form a fine firm bond with human beings. If puppies are removed from their litters too early or too late, behavior problems can develop.

An example of this is Macduff, a Scottish Terrier purchased from a mass-production kennel business. He was five months old when he was purchased by his owner, Joann. Joann called me because Macduff wouldn't come to her— ever. He never approached her when they were in the house. He actively avoided all her attempts to get him inside when she let Macduff out in her fenced backyard. Joann, a single woman, had recently lost an old dog and was bitterly disappointed by the lack of affection and responsiveness in her new Scottie. Macduff's behavior was the result of having been kept in a kennel isolated from people for too long. He was past the age when a puppy can best form a strong bond to humans. Fortunately, training the positive way helped him develop a relationship with his new owner, but it is unlikely that their relationship will fulfill all the potential it would have had if he had left the kennel at an earlier age.

Many personality traits that a dog will have when mature can be observed in a young puppy. Puppy behavior testing is a way of systematically making these observations. Seven weeks of age is a good time for this testing, because puppies at this age are physically mature enough to be able to move around easily, but young enough to make environmental influences on the puppy's behavior minimal. The testing should be done by someone who is a stranger to the puppies. Each puppy is tested individually, because puppies behave differently when separated from their littermates. The testing should also be done in a place that is strange to the puppies, to test their reactions to a new location.

Although someone experienced with puppy behavior testing would do the best job of testing, especially interpreting the puppies' behavior, you can do the testing yourself. Several tests are provided, as well as information on how to administer and interpret them. Make photocopies of tests, with one copy for each puppy, and circle the responses. The responses may not always be listed. Try to interpret these as best you can.

If you already have a dog, think about how your dog might have reacted to these tests as a puppy, and what that tells you about him now.

Puppy Behavior Tests

1. *Social Attraction*

   Have someone place the puppy on the floor approximately four feet from the tester, who is kneeling on the floor. The tester coaxes the puppy to him with his voice and body motions.

   Responses:

   A. Puppy runs to tester with tail up, jumps up.
   B. Puppy takes a few seconds to look around, then comes to tester, tail up.
   C. Puppy comes hesitantly, tail down.
   D. Puppy will not come at all; remains frozen in place.
   E. Puppy wanders off to explore room, ignoring tester.

   Meanings:

   A. This puppy is bold and confident. He likes people. Will you mind a problem with your dog jumping up on people? Don't be taken in by this attractive response. Bold dogs are difficult to control.
   B. Moderate response.
   C. Puppy is less sure of himself, especially in a strange place, but still attracted to people. May be easier to control. See if pup's confidence increases as test progresses.
   D. Puppy is scared, intolerant of stress. Look for trembling to indicate degree of fear. This puppy may be shy of strangers.
   E. There may be two reasons for this response. One is that the puppy is not a people-oriented dog, preferring to satisfy his own curiosity than to seek company. His independence may make him hard to train. The other reason for this response is that the puppy is not attracted to strangers, but may still bond well to one person.

2. *Following*

   The tester stands up and walks away from the puppy, talking to the puppy encouragingly. Walk about ten to twenty feet, if there is room.

   Responses:

   A. Follows readily, tail up, gets underfoot or runs ahead.
   B. Follows readily, tail up.
   C. Follows hesitantly, tail down.
   D. Does not follow; remains frozen in place.
   E. Wanders off to explore.

   Meanings:

   A. While attracted to people, this puppy is also assertive. May need an equally assertive owner.
   B. Confident, but ready to follow owner, literally and figuratively.
   C. Puppy less confident.

This seven-week-old puppy is demonstrating his attraction to people on the social attraction part of puppy behavior testing.   (Labrador Retriever)

The restraint test.   (Labrador Retriever)

D. Puppy scared.

E. This puppy is independent and will be difficult to establish control of off leash.

3. *Restraint*

The tester gently places the puppy on his back and holds him there for thirty seconds.

Responses:

A. Puppy struggles fiercely, bites.
B. Puppy struggles fiercely, may bark.
C. Puppy struggles a little.
D. Puppy does not struggle, relaxed.
E. Puppy does not struggle, tense.

Meanings:

A. Avoid this puppy if you have small children. Many children are bitten when they are restraining their dog by hugging him. This dog may be hard to restrain at the veterinarian. Early and firm training will be necessary.
B. Indicates active, assertive dog, lacking in tolerance.
C. Moderate response.
D. This more passive, easygoing pup will be easier to handle.
E. Puppy scared, stressed.

4. *Reaction to Petting*

The tester sits the puppy beside him and pets the puppy, talks to him.

Responses:

A. Puppy climbs or attempts to climb up on tester's lap; jumps at face and licks.
B. Puppy cuddles up to tester.
C. Puppy sits quietly, accepting petting.
D. Puppy crouches down, trembles.
E. Puppy goes around tester, sniffing shoes, or goes away.

Meanings:

A. The puppy loves people, but are his constant attempts to climb into your lap (and maybe everyone else's) or otherwise get your attention going to bother you? Will you enjoy it?
B. An affectionate puppy.
C. This puppy either isn't friendly with strangers or is still a little scared.
D. Puppy is scared.
E. Puppy is not attracted to people and independent.

5. *Retrieving*

The tester crumples up a piece of paper and tosses it two to four feet in front of the puppy while he is looking. If he picks it up, encourage him to come back.

Responses:

A. Chases paper, grabs it, and runs off.
B. Chases paper, sniffs it, runs off.
C. Chases paper, picks it up, and returns to tester.
D. Approaches paper hestitantly, stretches nose to cautiously sniff paper.
E. Chases paper a short distance, but returns to tester.
F. Not interested; wanders off.
G. Refuses to leave tester.

Meanings:

A. Puppy may always chase things he sees, like dogs on the other side of the road. He is also exhibiting independence.
B. Same as above, with less retrieving instinct.
C. Good response; retrieving correlated with high trainability.
D. Puppy lacks confidence, but may retrieve with practice and encouragement; may also indicate pointing ability in bird-hunting dog.
E. Indicates high level of social attraction and less retrieving instinct.
F. No retrieving instinct, puppy will probably not play retrieving games; indicates independence and reduced trainability.
G. Puppy scared.

6. *Touch Sensitivity*

The tester cradles the puppy in lap, takes webbing between front toes between thumb and forefinger, and gradually increases pressure while counting to ten. Stop as soon as the puppy pulls his paw away.

Meaning:

Some dogs are more pain sensitive than others. Dogs that are not pain sensitive may be hard to train by traditional methods that rely on dog's discomfort. A common problem with such dogs is pulling on the leash. Other dogs may be pain sensitive and overreact to every touch, perhaps nipping when a hair gets pulled while being brushed. A middle response is desirable. Most dogs are relatively pain insensitive.

7. *Sound Sensitivity*

The tester hits the bottom of a metal pan with a metal spoon while the puppy is a few feet away. Set the pan on the ground after hitting it.

Responses:

A. Puppy locates sound and trots to pan to investigate.

This puppy's response to the retrieving test indicates he will have a high level of trainability.

It is normal for a puppy to be startled when an umbrella is opened in the sight sensitivity test. (Labrador Retriever)

B. Puppy looks toward direction of sound but doesn't walk toward pan.

C. Puppy cringes, runs away, and tries to hide.

Meanings:

A. Puppy is bold and confident, not sound shy.

B. Puppy is less bold, but not sound shy.

C. Degree of fear shown indicates degree of sound shyness, sometimes called gun shyness. Even if you don't hunt, this fear can cause problems, like fear of thunderstorms or running away when a car backfires.

8. *Sight Sensitivity*

The tester opens an umbrella held close to ground about four feet away from the puppy and sets the umbrella on ground.

Responses:

A. Puppy may or may not jump back, but then approaches umbrella on own; may mouth umbrella.

B. Puppy may or may not jump back; approaches umbrella with encouragement.

C. Puppy cringes, goes away, and tries to hide.

Meanings:

A. Puppy very bold and curious, not afraid of things.

B. Puppy less bold but not afraid.

C. Puppy afraid of strange-looking objects; often grows up to be a dog easily "spooked."

9. *Energy Level*

Tester observes puppy during testing.

Responses:

A. Mostly runs about, never stops.

B. Mostly trots, mildly curious.

C. Walks quietly about, remains in position tester puts him in.

D. Moves very little, tense.

Meanings:

A. High energy level. Will be hard to keep quiet and will need a *lot* of exercise.

B. Medium energy level. Will still need exercise.

C. Low energy level. Easy to live with.

D. Puppy scared, stressed.

This ten-week-old puppy is learning to sit with food. (Basset Hound)

STARTING TRAINING

Training starts the minute you bring your puppy home. Communication begins immediately, whether it is part of a carefully planned training program or not. Your puppy is learning from all his interactions with you, and by planning your training from the start, you can make sure you and your puppy develop the relationship you want to have. Between the ages of seven and twelve weeks you have a great opportunity to get your training off to a good start. This training will revolve around housebreaking (covered in the previous chapter), teaching commands, dealing with annoying puppy behaviors (like mouthing your hands and grabbing everything not nailed down to the floor), starting off-leash training, building your dog's confidence, and initiating street training.

TEACHING COMMANDS: SIT, STAY, OKAY, AND NO

Training to teach specific words should begin at about eight to nine weeks of age. This training will set the tone of your relationship right from the beginning. Your puppy will learn to enjoy training, and the positive nature of this training will counteract the effects of other corrections you will be making as you raise your puppy. Your puppy will also learn that you will be communicating with him with words and signals, and that he will be rewarded for paying attention and responding.

Start with a hungry, alert puppy and a lot of treats. These treats should be very small in size, so that your puppy will not get filled up quickly, and should be something soft that he can easily eat. Good examples would be hot dogs sliced into pieces the size of a nickel and then cut again into quarters, or semimoist cat treats. Start training in a place where your puppy will not be distracted.

You will immediately notice a benefit of using food: you have your puppy's attention! The first command you will teach is "Sit." You can do this training either standing or kneeling beside your puppy. Your puppy will be standing, most likely dancing around trying to get at the food. Take a piece of food in your right hand and hold it so that it is almost touching your puppy's nose. For now, it is okay if he is chewing on your fingers. Say your dog's name to get his attention, then give the command to sit: "Max, sit." Say it in a pleasant tone of voice. Then move your right hand backward over your dog's head so he tips his head back and falls backward into a sitting position. If he doesn't sit right away, keep trying until he does. You shouldn't have to touch Max at all, but if you are really having problems, gently push his rump downwith your left hand. Ignore any attempts Max makes to jump up and get the food, and don't give it to him until he sits with all four paws on the floor. He will soon figure out, without your punishing him, that jumping up won't get him the food. He will also be learning the hand signal to sit, which is the same hand motion you have been making, minus the food.

Soon your puppy will be following you around and sitting, as described in the first chapter. Everyone in your family should learn how to do this, even young children. It helps to have kids keep the piece of food closed in a fist until the puppy sits, and then open their hands flat to give it to him. In this way they won't get their fingers chewed.

The next exercise will teach your dog several things. In addition to teaching him the meaning of the words "stay," "no," and "okay," your puppy will be learning to accept restraint, a very important lesson.

Start this exercise by kneeling beside your puppy. Have two pieces of food in your hand. Tell him to sit, preferably on your left side, and make the hand signal he has already learned. Reward him with one piece of food. Then, while you restrain him with one hand, put a piece of food in front of him, about one foot away. It may be easier to have someone else place the food in front of him at first, so that your hands are free. In a firm tone of voice, tell him "Stay." Restrain him by placing your right hand on his chest and your left hand on his rump. You should be able to keep him in a sitting position this way.

If your puppy tries to get up before you say "Okay," say "No, sit." Some puppies may frantically struggle against the restraint. If your puppy does, give him a little shake while keeping your hands in place and say "No." There is no reason to become more forceful; simply be more stubborn than he is. When he gives up and stops struggling, say "Okay" and release him, indicating to him that he can eat the piece of food on the ground, and praise him.

You want your puppy to understand that "No" means to stop doing whatever he is doing, and that "Okay" means that he is released from the previous command. If you are going to teach your dog to stay, he has to have a word that means the end of the stay. For instance, you want to be able to tell your dog to stay when you open the car door and not get out until you say "Okay." You don't want the release command to be "Good dog" or a hand motion. You want to be able to praise your dog without releasing him. "Good dog" should mean "I like what you are doing; keep doing it." An example of this would be if your dog was lying down and staying while you had company. You would want to be able to praise him without having him get up. If you use some sort of movement to release your dog, then anytime you moved when he was staying, he would jump up.

Accepting restraint is important for dogs to learn. It is important not only for teaching them to stay, but also for accepting restraint when receiving veterinary care and grooming, and even accepting the restraint of a small child hugging them. Dogs who do not accept restraint often bite when restraint is attempted. A problem with restraint can mean that the veterinarian cannot draw a blood sample for a heartworm test or look at an infected ear. It can mean that a long-haired dog becomes a matted mess because he cannot be brushed. At its worst, it can result in a child with a scarred face because she put her arms around a dog's neck and hugged him. Starting early with this simple exercise is a good way to prevent these problems.

Practice this exercise until your puppy will stay without your having to hold him in position. Gradually increase the length of time he will stay. Make him stay when you give him his dinner. Anyone who has had a dog jump up and hit a bowl full of dog food and send it flying all over the kitchen will appreciate the value of this training. Make your puppy stay until the bowl is on the floor, then wait a few seconds before you release him with an "Okay" to eat his food. Again, every member of the family should be able to do this.

Once these two exercises are mastered, you can proceed with the rest of the training detailed in Chapter 5.

HANDLING PUPPY BEHAVIOR PROBLEMS THE POSITIVE WAY

Puppies seem to be in perpetual trouble. One minute your little puppy terrorist is jumping up and biting at your hands while you are trying to read the newspaper; a few minutes later you find him chewing on the fringe of the oriental carpet. Next he is racing through the house with one of the kid's stuffed animals in his mouth, being chased by the tearful owner of the toy and defying capture. Then he suddenly stops and relieves himself on the carpet. What do you do?

Punishment is not the answer. As annoying as all these behaviors are, they are all normal puppy behaviors. It isn't fair to punish a puppy for engaging in normal puppy behaviors before you have given him time to learn the rules for living in human society. Punishment would only confuse him and make him afraid of you. Remember, we are talking about a seven- to twelve-week-old puppy.

The real answer requires understanding, prevention, training, and time. Puppyhood is a temporary state. The razor-sharp needle teeth will fall out. Your puppy will eventually have tasted everything in your house and will be bored with it. He'll calm down, at least a little. He'll hopefully learn the rules. Meanwhile, you want to prevent damage, distract him from getting into trouble, and tire him out with plenty of exercise.

Mouthing upsets and scares many puppy owners because it seems aggressive. People expect a fuzzy bundle of love when they get a puppy, not a tiny alligator with hair. However, mouthing is a perfectly normal puppy behavior. It is how puppies and even adult dogs play with each other—they chew on each other. So a puppy mouthing you is only attempting to play with you in the way that is most natural to him. With age, and a little mild discouragement, the little needle teeth fall out and the puppy learns that mouthing is not an acceptable form of play with humans.

A dog that tends to mouth a lot and a small child can be a difficult combination. Puppies tend to view small kids as littermates and play with them accordingly. This can be very frightening to a child who is not much bigger than the dog. Try kneeling and fending off a rambunctious puppy from that height. It's not easy. Parents need to teach their children to behave appropriately around the puppy, such as not running through the house and roughhousing with the puppy. Parents also need to firmly discipline the puppy for nipping at the kids.

If things get so bad that your three-year-old is taking refuge from the puppy by climbing on the kitchen table, or your five-year-old's clothing is being torn, you need to take further action. Fill a spray bottle or plant mister with a fifty-fifty mixture of water and white distilled vinegar. Instruct your child to say "No" when the puppy grabs at him and then spray the puppy in his face. The vinegar will not hurt his eyes. Do not allow your child access to the spray bottle unless you are directly supervising him. The spray bottle will eliminate the chance of provoking a defensive reaction from the puppy. Never allow your child to hit your puppy.

Preventing damage is done by limiting your puppy's freedom. As with housebreaking, do not let him have free run of your home. Keep doors to rooms shut. Just as a baby is put in a playpen for his own safety when he cannot be watched, confine your puppy when he cannot be watched. The use of crates and exercise pens is discussed in Chapter 2. Teach your kids to pick up their toys and your husband to pick up his socks.

Damage control also means puppy-proofing your home. For example, to deal with a puppy that is chewing the fringe on the oriental carpet, roll up the carpet and put it away until the puppy is older. You could also tuck the fringe under the carpet and tape it there. Another tactic would be to spray the fringe with something the puppy won't like the taste of, such as Grannick's Bitter Apple spray (available in dog supply stores and catalogues). Apply this kind of creative problem solving to whatever problems you are having.

When your puppy grabs something he shouldn't have and runs around the house with it, do not make the multiple mistakes of chasing him, wrestling whatever it is out of his mouth, and then punishing him. All these actions will make the problem worse. Chasing him is exactly what your puppy wants, so you are rewarding him and thus making it more likely that he will repeat the behavior in the future—exactly what you don't want. You'll find him grabbing things just to get your attention. Instead, try to get him to come to you. It helps if your dog is trained to come when called, as described in Chapter 6. You might want to wait a few seconds before calling him to give him a chance to discover that nobody is going to chase him. Don't use a threatening or angry tone of voice. Entice him to you with a treat if necessary, exchanging the treat for whatever he has in his mouth. This problem is especially difficult if you have young children who are all too anxious to join in the catch-me-if-you-can game. A family conference at which everyone promises not to chase the dog if he has something in his mouth is a good idea.

Trying to pull something out of your puppy's mouth is again rewarding a behavior you don't want. Just as playing chasing games is a normal puppy play behavior, so is playing tug-of-war, so these behaviors are easy to encourage unintentionally. Pulling on something will encourage him to hang on harder. To get your puppy to release something, apply pressure with your thumb and forefinger on both sides of your dog's muzzle, pressing his lips against his teeth. At

Be sure to make eye contact when doing a scruff shake. (Shetland Sheepdog)

the same time, give your dog the command "Drop it." He will learn to drop things when you just touch the side of his mouth, and eventually on command. Don't forget to praise him for releasing the object.

Punishing your dog in this situation will only make him less likely to come to you next time. He will grab something, then run off and hide, where you won't discover he is destroying it until it is too late. If you cannot tell him "No" when he is thinking about grabbing something, it is too late to punish.

While a tug-of-war is not good when you are trying to get something out of your puppy's mouth, it is a good game to play with your puppy to use up some of his energy. It is a good substitute when your puppy wants to play by chewing on your hands or tugging on your clothing. You can use something as simple as an old towel or the leg cut off an old pair of jeans. Make sure your puppy will release whatever you are using on command, and do not allow the game to become too aggressive. It is also a good way to practice your "Drop it" command.

Distracting a puppy with lots of toys is a good technique to prevent damage and to use up puppy energy. Instead of giving him all the toys at once, try giving him only two toys at a time, then exchange them for two new ones when he becomes bored. Seven- to twelve-week-old puppies need soft toys because they do not have adult teeth and will soon be losing their baby teeth. Toys that would be dangerous to give them as adult dogs are safe now, such as a piece of fake fur cloth that he can pretend to kill. Sometimes the best toys are as simple as a knotted rope, a cardboard paper towel roll, or an empty plastic bottle.

If prevention, distraction, and a sharp "No!" do not work, discipline will be necessary. The best way to do this is with a scruff shake. This will effectively and humanely get his attention. First, get a good hold on your puppy. Do not yell at him as you approach him or he will run away. If he does run, do not wildly chase him through the house. Simply walk after him quietly until you have him cornered. Once you have hold of him, if he is small, pick him up by the scruff of the neck, which is the extra skin on the back of his neck, and hold him so you are looking into his eyes. If he is too large to pick up, lift his front feet off the ground. Say a few words, like "Stop it" or "Knock it off," in a low-pitched, authoritative tone of voice. Maintain eye contact while you are doing this. Keep your puppy elevated until he is no longer struggling and you feel his muscles relax. Then put him back down and reassure him *just a little* that you still love him. You should be forceful enough to make your point, but not so much that you terrify him.

Some puppies do bite aggressively, which is an entirely different matter than playful mouthing. If your puppy growls or snaps when you try to take something away from him, when you try to move him when he is sleeping, when you try to restrain him, or when a stranger tries to pet him, all these instances require immediate and very firm discipline as described above. Read more about aggression in Chapter 9 and, if the biting continues, obtain the help of a dog trainer experienced in handling such problems.

Never hit your puppy with your hand or an object. It generally just causes

Be realistic about the possibility of some damage occurring while raising a puppy.

your puppy to get more excited and may trigger a defensive response on his part if he interprets the hitting as an attack. Don't verbally abuse him, either. Loud screaming will undermine his trust in you.

Exercise is a great way of dealing with all puppy behavior problems. A tired puppy gets into less trouble. Puppies need frequent, short bursts of exercise. One way of tiring out a puppy is having two people stand fifty feet or more apart and call the puppy back and forth between them, giving the puppy a treat each time he comes. You will be teaching your puppy to come when called and tiring him out at the same time. We had fun with our Greyhound puppy by tying an old dust mop cover to a piece of string and letting her chase it. I'd hold her while my husband took off running, dragging the dust mop behind him. When he was far enough ahead, I'd release her to chase after him. The walks you will be taking as part of your off-leash training will also help. And one of the best ways to tire out a puppy is to give him a chance to play with another puppy.

Be realistic. Some damage is probably going to be done while you are raising a puppy, in spite of your best efforts to prevent it. A magazine may be ripped up, trash may be strewn all over the floor, and you may get a nasty scratch from puppy teeth. If you can't handle this without getting angry, think twice about bringing a puppy into your home. Even if you are looking at your most expensive pair of shoes in tatters on the floor, remember that he is just a puppy and try to laugh. Losing your temper is a waste of energy. It won't bring your shoes back. And remember, you left them where he could get at them.

Enjoy your puppy's antics. I laugh now at the memory of Zephyr, my Greyhound, who jumped in the car while I was unloading my groceries, grabbed a package of rolls, and took off through the woods at top speed, leaving a trail of rolls behind her. Although it may not seem so at the time, you'll miss the puppy games after they grow up.

BUILDING CONFIDENCE

Building your dog's confidence is an important part of getting off to a good start. Dogs start to develop their attitudes toward people and the outside world as soon as they can see and hear, so exposing a puppy to people and places to build his confidence around them, often called *socialization*, should begin as soon as you get him, ideally at seven weeks. Your dog should be confident with people of all sizes and shapes and in new situations and places. If this exposure does not start before a dog is twelve weeks old, your dog may have confidence problems. He may be afraid of people or afraid when you take him to new places. He won't be happy, and neither will you.

Start by introducing your puppy to lots of different people—children and babies, tall people, fat people, men with beards, and women with large hats. He should meet these people both at your house and in other places.

If your puppy shows fear of anyone, be careful not to inadvertently praise him for being fearful. This happens when an owner tries to reassure a frightened puppy by petting him and speaking soothingly to him. Unfortunately, the puppy thinks that you are praising him for acting fearful and will act more fearful in the future. Fearful behavior can then progress to growling and snapping. Don't misinterpret this as overprotectiveness on the part of your dog. Your dog is simply afraid, and has been encouraged to act that way by you. The proper response to fearfulness is to insist your puppy not back away from whatever frightens him. The sit-stay (see Chapter 5) is a useful tool in dealing with this situation. In a firm but kind voice, tell your dog to stop acting silly. Then have the person of whom your puppy is afraid offer him a bit of food. Try to make the puppy take a step forward to get the food. Then praise your dog for this behavior. If your puppy acts fearful of anything, don't avoid these situations or people with your puppy. Instead, try more exposure. Be careful, however, not to create such panic in your puppy that his fears are just further reinforced. You can push a little, but not too much.

A typical example is Tiki, a Yorkshire terrier. Tiki was enrolled in my obedience classes when her biting problem worsened. This is not unusual in small dogs, because it is easier to tolerate biting in them. When Tiki walked into the first class and I went to greet her, she hid behind her owner, who promptly picked her up and started cooing words of reassurance in Tiki's fringed ear. With that kind of backup, Tiki then turned into a miniature canine terrorist, snarling and growling at me. After I explained to Tiki's owner the effects of her reassurance, we started a program of building Tiki's confidence. I sat on the floor and offered Tiki, who was not in her owner's arms, a delectable tidbit of cooked beef liver seasoned with garlic powder. At first, she would only come as far as my outstretched arm. Gradually, I coaxed her closer, until she would finally climb into my lap. After a few weeks in class, we started to have the other class members offer Tiki a treat. We made sure Tiki was hungry and therefore motivated. It became a ritual after class; everyone fed Tiki before leaving. Meanwhile, Tiki was receiving the same treatment at home. By the end of the class, Tiki was running to greet people.

Some people are afraid to encourage friendliness in their dogs because they want their dogs to be protective. However, only a confident dog, a dog that is not afraid of people, can be counted on in a threatening situation. Socialization is absolutely necessary to help a dog distinguish between who is threatening and who is not. Protective behavior, if your dog has such instincts, will not emerge until your dog matures. If you see aggressive behavior in a puppy under six months of age, you can be sure it is caused by fear. Do something about it immediately.

Besides exposing your dog to different people to build his confidence, you will also want to take him to different places. Check with your veterinarian regarding when a puppy's vaccinations will provide him with adequate protection from infectious diseases. Meanwhile, take him to places where he wouldn't be exposed to such diseases. City dogs should go to the country, and suburban dogs should visit the city. Don't just take him to outdoor places. Ask a good friend to let your puppy come inside his house—on leash, of course! If the weather is warm, puppies can learn to swim at eight to ten weeks of age. Take it slowly; wade into the water and support your puppy. Remember, the idea is to build his confidence, not to scare him.

A good rule of thumb is to expose your puppy to anything he may face in his life before he is sixteen weeks old. Be creative. How about elevators, open staircases, wheelchairs, and baby strollers? An overnight stay at the boarding kennel where you plan to leave your dog when you go away is a good idea while he's still a puppy. Your puppy should have a chance to interact with other dogs. Puppy training classes are an excellent way to provide your puppy with exposure to different people, dogs, and places. (For more information on choosing a good training class, see Chapter 10.)

Taking the time to do this confidence building while your puppy is still young will give you many years of enjoying a confident dog. Your dog will be more adaptable and flexible. He will be better behaved when he meets new people or goes somewhere. If your dog is older, he will still benefit from such exposure, although progress may be slower.

STARTING OFF-LEASH TRAINING

Seven to twelve weeks of age is the perfect time to start your off-leash training. In fact, it is almost the only time. This time is so critical because during these weeks most puppies will instinctively stay close to their owners. After twelve weeks, dogs become more independent and more likely to stray.

Dogs not given the experience of off-leash freedom at this age will be much more difficult to train to obey when off leash later. By starting now, you can avoid the vicious cycle caused by lack of off-leash exercise. Dogs caught in this cycle build up energy and frustration, so they run away when they are finally off leash; this in turn makes it less likely that their owners will give them off-leash freedom, and the dog's frustration gets even worse.

It is best to never develop a dependence on the leash for control in the first place. While you should accustom your puppy to walking on leash, try to give him as much off-leash freedom as possible. If it isn't safe to allow your puppy to run free in your yard, take your puppy someplace where he can safely be off leash during this time period. Even if you have a fenced yard where your puppy can be off leash, you should still take him to someplace different, so you both get the feeling of off-leash freedom. Do this even if it means driving a distance. An advantage of going someplace different is that your puppy will naturally be more insecure and pay more attention to where you are. Just put your puppy down and start walking. Do not constantly call to him; you want to establish in him the habit of keeping track of where you are without your having to call him all the time. Several times during each walk, call your puppy to you, give him a treat, and turn him loose with an "Okay" to run some more. Always carry treats with you when your puppy is being exercised off leash, so you can reward him for coming.

Taking your young puppy for walks off leash is wonderful for getting your relationship off to a good start. (Basset Hound)

These off-leash walks will have a special effect on your relationship with your dog. They strengthen your emotional ties in a magical way. It is almost as if you are re-creating the times when wild canines struck off on the hunt together. In any case, there are few activities a dog enjoys more than a chance to be free to run and explore. Even if off-leash control is not important to you, I recommend these walks for the bond they create between you and your dog.

Once you've gotten your off-leash training off to a good start, continue teaching your puppy to come when called as described in Chapters 5 and 6.

STREET TRAINING

Accidents happen. A guest at your house may mistakenly let your dog out the front door. A child may open the gate to your fenced yard and let your dog loose. Many dogs are killed every year when they are hit by cars. You can help prevent this from happening to your dog by training your puppy not to go into the street. This is street training.

It is critical that this training be done when your puppy is between the ages of eight to ten weeks. This is because the training is based on creating in your dog a fear of the street, and a puppy of this age is very susceptible to forming permanent fears if he is badly frightened. And that is exactly what you will be doing—frightening your puppy. This training is not done with positive reinforcement, and it is certainly not fun for you or your puppy, but the results are worthwhile.

The training takes two people, one to handle the puppy, and another person to stand in the street and look for cars. You will probably want to have your puppy on a long, lightweight piece of rope, about thirty feet in length. One person, the spotter, should go down the driveway to the road in front of the house where the puppy lives. He should cross to the opposite side of the street and go down the road about twenty feet from the driveway. When there is no traffic coming in either direction, he should indicate that it is clear by yelling to you, the puppy's handler.

You should be waiting in the driveway, about ten feet from the end of the driveway, holding on to the puppy's collar. When your spotter indicates it is clear, release the puppy, letting him drag the long line, and walk toward the road. Do not hold on to the line. Do not attempt to stop or slow down your puppy as he approaches the street. Hopefully he will walk ahead of you and proceed into the street. If the puppy does not immediately go into the street, you should stop about five feet from the road and wait until he wanders into the road. Prior to starting out, you should decide where you are going to establish the line your dog shouldn't cross. This is obvious if you have a curb along the road where you live, but if not, you'll have to pick a boundary line.

When your puppy crosses that line, start screaming at the top of your lungs in the most dramatic way possible. It doesn't matter what words you say, as long as your tone of voice indicates fear. Most puppies will respond by crouching down. If your puppy doesn't run back toward you, you should run to the puppy, using the light line to restrain him if he starts to run away. The older the puppy, the more likely it is that he will try to run away when you scream. The unfortunate truth is that most puppies learn as they get older to associate your raised voice with imminent punishment.

When you reach your puppy, stop screaming, scoop him up into your arms, and run to "safety," about ten to fifteen feet back from the road. Tell your puppy how lucky he was to be rescued from the jaws of death. Put him down and hug him and reassure him. It is important that your puppy not be afraid of you, so keep reassuring him so he huddles against you for protection. The idea is not to punish your puppy, but to have him think terrible things happen when he steps into the street.

If you are sufficiently dramatic the first time, your puppy may refuse to go near the street, even if you walk toward it. Praise him for staying back from the street, and call it quits for the day. If your puppy willingly goes into the street again, repeat your performance with more intensity. If it helps you get into your role, picture your puppy crushed and dead in the road.

The next day, try it again. Make sure you have a spotter. This time add temptations that might induce your puppy to go into the street. Have your spotter or your kids jog along the opposite side of the road. Laughing and talking are fine, but they may not call your puppy's name. Toss a stick or stone into the street. If your puppy succumbs to the temptation, react as you did before.

Some puppies, especially those that are of a submissive nature, may become very fearful of the street, so that even if you attempt to cross the street with them on a leash, they will pull back with all their strength. That's okay. Try to avoid crossing the street, if possible. If you must cross the street, pick up your puppy and carry him across. Do not walk your puppy in the street to exercise him for several months. Drive to someplace to exercise him, if necessary.

Practice approaching the street daily. All too often people prevent their dogs from ever getting near the street, and then when their dogs escape from their control, the dogs don't have any training to prevent them from running into the street. If your mailbox is down near the road, take your dog with you when you go to get your mail. When you walk your dog, make him sit and wait before crossing the street. Then give him a release command, like "Okay." If you walk in an area where there are no sidewalks and you must walk your dog in the street, make a big production of crossing the boundary line you have established. I live in an area with no sidewalks, and my husband jogs in the street with the dogs to exercise them. In spite of their frequent exposure to being in the street, they understand they are not to go into the street *on their own*.

Once your puppy has learned to stay away from the street in front of your house, repeat the street training in at least three different places. After this your puppy will understand that he is to stay out of *all* streets, not just the street in front of your house. A benefit of street training is that your dog will more readily learn boundaries.

When your dog gets older, his inhibitions will undoubtedly decrease as his

Let your puppy approach the street. Do not give him any verbal warnings.

As soon as your puppy steps into the street, swoop down on him, screaming.   (Basset Hound)

66

curiosity and confidence grow. The training will have to be reinforced. At this point, you will probably be unable to frighten your dog, so the training is more like punishment. Again, set up the situation so you have control over the circumstances. Have a spotter to tell you when there are no cars coming. Have available whatever might entice your dog to step into the street. Your dog must be on a long leash. You might want to play with him in the yard with the long leash on for a few minutes beforehand so that he forgets about being on the long leash. When he steps into the street, pounce on him and let loose the full extent of your fury, shaking him and screaming rather than hitting him. Be very dramatic.

We are responsible for keeping our dogs in an environment that is full of dangers they can't understand, like fast-moving cars. It is therefore our responsibility to protect them to the best of our ability. While a leash is the best protection against dogs being hit by cars, dogs still manage to get loose, and there are many benefits to off-leash exercise. If you are going to give your dog any off-leash freedom in a unfenced area, street training is a must. Taking the time to do this training, even though the training is not pleasant for you or your puppy, is cheap insurance.

Dogs bred to hunt, like this German Shorthaired Pointer, need a lot of exercise.

4

Understanding
Your Dog's Personality

To FORM A GOOD RELATIONSHIP with your dog, you have
to have two-way communication. The following chapter will be about training
your dog to understand your language in the form of commands. First, however,
you need to learn to understand your dog. This mutual understanding is critical
for effective training and to establish a good relationship.

Personalities are what make dogs so fascinating, and they are all different.
Each dog is unique. Your dog's personality will affect his training, so it is
important to understand some of the factors that make up a dog's personality.
Many of the factors are hereditary; as such, they cannot be easily changed and
are best handled with a strong dose of understanding.

BEHAVIORS RELATED TO BREED

Most breeds were developed to do a specific job. An important part in
understanding your dog is to research what job he was bred for and recognize
how that affects his behavior as your pet. Although few pure-bred dogs are still
performing whatever job they were bred to do, the behaviors remain. To confuse
the issue, these behaviors remain in varying strength. An infamous example is
the Irish Setter, which has been bred for its beauty for so long that some have lost
their ability to find birds. However, few seem to have lost their desire to run.
Keep in mind as you are reading this that these are generalizations that will not
apply to all individuals within a breed.

Understanding how your dog's breed affects his behavior can be a challenge if your dog is a mixed breed. These dogs are often misunderstood because they don't have a breed identity to lead to an understanding of their behavior. Try to guess what breeds may be combined in your mixed-breed dog. Judge by characteristics like shape of ear, tail carriage, size, and coat rather than by color. Stick to the more popular breeds, as they are more likely to be part of a mixed breeding. It is unlikely that your dog is a cross between an Ibizan Hound and a Wirehaired Pointing Griffon.

Many breeds of dogs were developed to hunt in different ways that affect their behavior as pets. Some dogs hunt by sight, while others hunt by smell. Beagles, when off leash, are easily distracted by smells on the ground; Afghan Hounds are more likely to be distracted by something they see moving. Terriers were bred to hunt small rodents, which were sometimes not much smaller than they were. This produced a feisty dog that is eager to do battle and is not afraid of anything. Setters hunt by covering a lot of ground, and they will often do exactly that when allowed off leash.

An important factor that affects how easy it is to train your dog is whether or not his breed was developed to work in close cooperation with man or independently of him. For example, both the Golden Retriever and the Border Collie were bred to take directions from humans to do their job. On the other hand, when Beagles are working as hunters, they do not wait for instructions from their handlers, but strike off on their own, looking for rabbit scent. Setters and Pointers fall somewhere in between, searching independently for game birds, but staying within range of the hunter with whom they are working.

Some dogs were bred to hunt or work for long periods of time, such as Setters, Pointers, and Border Collies. You shouldn't be surprised if your German Shorthaired Pointer, which was bred to hunt all day at a steady gallop, paces restlessly around the house and gets into trouble when he doesn't get enough exercise. On the other hand, people are often surprised to learn that some of the breeds bred to hunt by running down game, such as Greyhounds and Afghans, are content to sleep away the day rather than by running through the house. They were not bred to hunt all day at a steady pace, but to capture their prey in brief bursts of speed.

The behavior of dogs bred to herd, such as Collies and Shetland Sheepdogs, causes problems for many dog owners. It may mean that your Australian Shepherd obsessively rounds up the neighborhood kids in your backyard and won't allow them to move. Or it may mean that your Border Collie mix bites at the back of your legs when you try to walk. Herding breeds have an instinctive need to control moving objects. This works great if you have a herd of sheep you want to move, but poorly if the herding instinct is extended to small children or cars passing by. They are often compulsive retrievers, extending their herding instinct to balls or Frisbees. This herding behavior can be confused with an aggressive attack, and indeed the line between the two can sometimes be hard to draw. If you have a herding breed or mix, it would be wise to expose him to things like groups of small children running around and make sure he understands that under no circumstances is he to chase them.

These breed-related behaviors are instinctive, and they cannot be erased by training, only understood and controlled. Keep in mind that often these behaviors are at their worst in a bored dog. Terriers will dig, Huskies will howl, and Border Collies will chase cars. Training, stimulation, and exercise are all helpful.

Now we will examine some inherited personality characteristics that affect all dogs, regardless of breed. While we will be discussing extremes of each characteristic, there is a continuous range of behavior between the extremes that might best describe your dog. It is important to note that these personality traits are not necessarily good or bad, but rather a matter of personal preference. Puppy behavior testing gives a good indication of these personality traits at an early age (see chapter 3).

Evaluating Your Dog's Personality

Understanding your dog's personality is important for successful training and a good relationship. Circle the description below that best fits your dog.

Personality Traits	High	Medium	Low
Assertiveness	Barks or paws at door when wants to go out	Sometimes whines when his dinner is late	Rarely asks to go out or begs for food
Defense reaction	Readily bites when stressed	Would bite if very frightened	Wouldn't bite even if very frightened
Dependence	Very upset when left alone; never runs away	Unhappy when left alone; wanders off, but not far	Would run away if given the chance
Energy level	Always ready to go; can't get enough exercise	Likes exercise, but no problem if day is missed	Sleeps most of the time; only needs short walks
Reactivity	Gets excited easily; high-strung	Barks or jumps up when people come but settles down	Calm; laid-back
Intelligence	Is always one step ahead of you; easily bored	Learns quickly but isn't creative	Isn't quick to learn or solve problems
Trainability	Does whatever you want; easy to train	Has some bad habits but tries to please	Very difficult to train; independent, assertive

ASSERTIVE AND PASSIVE DOGS

If you have a dog that is somewhat of a "problem child," chances are that you have an assertive dog. Assertive dogs are those that actively try to get their own way. Because of this, they are more difficult to handle than a passive dog that is willing to be a follower. The passive dog does not take the initiative. He is not a creative thinker, as the assertive dog is. Assertive dogs are the ones that learn to ask to go out to relieve themselves, while passive dogs do not. They bark to make sure you don't forget to feed them dinner. And why is it that some dogs steal food at any opportunity, while others never do? Again, it's the difference between an assertive and passive dog, rather than a difference in appetites. The passive dog is one that is obedient, even though he's never had any formal training. The assertive dog, even if he holds several obedience titles, is rarely described as obedient.

Note that there is a difference between assertiveness and aggression. A dog can be assertive without being aggressive, and a dog can be aggressive without being assertive. For instance, Sandy is a mixed Shepherd who snarls and snaps at anyone who approaches within five feet of her because she is afraid of people. She is a very timid dog that is scared of her own shadow. She is an aggressive dog, but she is certainly not assertive. On the other hand, Hayley is a Gordon Setter that is assertive, pawing at you constantly for attention and not taking no for an answer. She barks at the door when she wants to go out, which is approximately every fifteen minutes. If all else fails, she will steal something she knows she is not supposed to have and will run through the house with it—a sure attention-getter. However, one cannot imagine any circumstance in which Hayley would bite.

My Borzoi, Carla, was the epitome of an assertive dog. What Carla wanted in life was more food, and she would go to any length to get it. She learned to open cabinet doors in the kitchen, so we put child-proof locks on all those doors behind which food was kept. We live on the Appalachian Trail and are often visited by hikers. Carla learned to operate the zippers on their backpacks to steal their food. One of her more appalling stunts was the time she pushed open the door to a neighbor's home, walked in, stole a huge piece of Vermont cheddar cheese, and calmly strolled out, all while the dumbfounded neighbor looked on.

On the other hand, it would never enter Sabre's mind to jump up on a countertop and help himself to a piece of food, although he loves to eat just as much as Carla did and spent years watching her steal food. Sabre is a passive dog. We call him "The Boy Scout" because he never seems to do anything wrong. It isn't that he lies around the house doing nothing. He's a confident, energetic dog who is always ready for a game of Frisbee and is a great watchdog. He just doesn't take any initiative.

The passive dog is easier to live with, but there's a lot to be said for the surprises and entertainment an assertive dog can give you. Becoming equally assertive and developing a strong sense of humor may help you deal with this type of dog. Training is a must to set limits for the assertive dog, but don't expect to change his personality.

AGGRESSIVE OR PASSIVE DEFENSE REACTIONS

Whether or not a dog tends to bite when it is frightened or stressed is an inherited behavior. While all dogs can bite if severely stressed, some dogs resort to biting more quickly than others. These are dogs with aggressive defense reactions.

The different types of defense reactions are easy to observe in my obedience classes during the class in which we teach toenail clipping, because so many dogs are frightened or stressed by this procedure. A big male Golden Retriever may be totally terrified and struggling with all his might, but he does not bite. Meanwhile, an Airedale has bitten the hand of my assistant instructor for simply holding his paw.

These tendencies can be observed in puppies during puppy behavior testing at seven weeks of age when undergoing the restraint test. Puppies that are stressed by being held on their backs can react by freezing in fear or by the other extreme of growling and biting. However, some puppies are not stressed by being held on their backs and lie there quite relaxed, which brings up an important point. These puppies may or may not have aggressive defense reactions, but they are not easily stressed. Some dogs are more easily stressed than others, and this affects how easily a defense reaction of either type can be provoked. A dog with aggressive defense reactions that is easily stressed can be very difficult to handle.

Aggressive or passive defense reactions are linked to a dog's breed. Obviously, dogs bred to be protective, such as German Shepherds and Dobermans, are also bred to have aggressive defense reactions. Retrievers, on the other hand, are bred to have "soft mouths" so they won't crush the birds they were bred to retrieve and consequently have passive defense reactions. Newfoundlands are another example of a breed that tends to have passive defense reactions. Unfortunately, the indiscriminate breeding of dogs has blurred many of these breed tendencies.

Dogs that show signs of aggressive defense reactions benefit from being trained as young as possible to accept restraint so they can be groomed and given veterinary care without biting. See Chapters 3 and 5 for instructions on how to do this.

When training a dog with aggressive defense reflexes, any kind of punishment or force that makes the dog feel a need to defend itself must be avoided. You don't want to give the dog practice at biting by provoking such a reaction. On the other hand, dogs with passive reactions are often victims of forceful training techniques because they do not defend themselves. Food training works well for both types of dogs.

Defense reactions are an important personality factor to keep in mind when

Some dogs will show passive defense reactions.

Others will show aggressive reactions to stressful situations.

choosing a dog that will be around children. If you have small children, it is safest to have a dog with passive defense reactions.

INDEPENDENT OR DEPENDENT

Dogs vary in how dependent they are on their human owners. Dogs are social animals, as are their wild counterparts, wolves. It is a dog's ability to form social attachments that makes him so desirable as a companion. All dogs need social contact to be happy, but some dogs are more stressed when denied that contact than others.

A gauge of a dog's independence is how he reacts to being left alone. The dependent dog is highly stressed in this situation and sometimes exhibits behavior problems such as barking, destructive chewing, and house soiling when left alone. He tries not to let you out of his sight when you are at home, following you from room to room.

The independent dog needs less human contact to be happy. He does not exhibit stress-related behavior when left alone, and while he is happy to see his owner return, he does not act as if he has been dying while his owner was gone. This is a useful trait for a dog that has to be left alone for long hours while his owners go to work.

Dependence is affected by both heredity and environmental factors. There are several different environmental factors. As a dog grows older, he usually becomes more independent. The presence of another dog provides social contact and decreases a dog's dependence on his owner.

A more complicated environmental factor revolves around the age at which a dog is removed from the litter. Dogs that are separated from their littermates before the age of six weeks are often more dependent, sometimes showing severe anxiety problems when separated from their owners. On the other hand, dogs that are not removed from the litter and exposed to human contact before twelve to sixteen weeks of age may not bond well to a human and therefore may be more independent.

The hereditary nature of dependence is indicated by breed tendencies. As a general rule, hounds (both sight and scent hounds), terriers, and the northern breeds are more independent. Chow Chows and Siberian Huskies are notorious examples of popular but independent breeds. Spaniels, retrievers, and herding breeds are more dependent. For instance, German Shepherds, Shetland Sheepdogs, and Golden Retrievers are examples of breeds generally having a dependent nature. Other breeds fall somewhere in between. When a breed was developed for doing a job that required submission to a human's direction, dependence was bred in as a desirable trait.

As with all personality traits, dependency affects training. Independence causes two main training problems. The first is that the independent dog is more difficult to motivate because he is not afraid of his owner's displeasure. In other words, he doesn't really care if he pleases his owner or not. While verbal praise

Dependent dogs cling to you for security.

Independent dogs are apt to take off on their own.

may motivate a dependent dog to obey his owner's command, it will not be sufficient motivation for an independent dog. Food rewards are good motivation for independent dogs. The other common training problem with an independent dog is that off-leash control is difficult to establish because the independent dog has no natural inclination to stay close to his owner.

Puppy behavior testing gives a good indication of a dog's degree of dependency. Puppies that keep wandering away from the tester between and during tests are showing independence.

ENERGY LEVEL AND REACTIVITY

As an obedience instructor, I frequently get complaints about "hyper" dogs. I've learned that this means one of four things: a perfectly normal dog that doesn't get enough exercise, a dog that has a high energy level, a highly reactive dog, or a hyperactive dog.

The high-energy dog is always ready to go. He doesn't tire easily, whether he's working or playing. The highly reactive dog may or may not have a high energy level, but he reacts strongly to stimuli. Stimulation overexcites him. If you touch him, he jumps away. If the doorbell rings, he becomes hysterical. He startles easily. In an exciting or stressful situation, he may tremble. Such dogs are often described as "nervous" or "high strung." If you were to open an umbrella in the face of a highly reactive dog, he would startle and jump back. A dog with a low reactivity level wouldn't even blink an eye.

Both high-energy and highly reactive dogs benefit from training. For the high-energy dog, it helps to use up some of his energy. The highly reactive dog benefits from being taught to control his reactions. Repeated exposure to different people, things, noises, and places will reduce reactivity. Both types of dog also benefit from more exercise.

The hyperactive dog is different from both of these. Hyperactivity is a neurological disorder. These dogs cannot slow down. They tend to learn poorly due to an inability to pay attention for any length of time. They often have multiple behavior problems. Training and exercise do not help much with these dogs. As with hyperactive children, they can be treated with drugs. The drugs used are not tranquilizers. Some veterinarians do not have much experience with this problem. If you suspect your dog is hyperactive, you will probably need the help of someone specializing in dog behavior problems. Some owners have reported improvement with dietary changes, such as eliminating preservatives from the diet.

INTELLIGENCE AND TRAINABILITY

Many dog owners are confused when their dogs seem to be intelligent but prove to be difficult to train. Intelligence and trainability are not the same thing.

The intelligent dog may be great at solving problems, but may not be the easiest dog to live with.

In fact, many dog trainers consider the more intelligent dog harder to train. Intelligence refers to a dog's ability to solve problems, while trainability is related to the ease with which a dog can be convinced to take direction from a human. A dog might use his intelligence to get what he wants, but he won't necessarily use it to do what you want.

It is interesting to note that most puppy behavior tests do not test for intelligence, but more for factors that affect trainability. Being able to train a dog is more important to how people get along with their dogs than intelligence.

Maggie was a mixed Shepherd that displayed a mixture of intelligence, independence, and assertiveness that frustrated her owner. Maggie learned to open the latch on the back door to let herself out of the house. She learned to listen for when her owner was in the bathroom so she could raid the garbage can. To help get some control, Maggie's owner enrolled both of them in a local obedience class. Maggie quickly learned all the exercises—heeling, sit-stay, lying down on command. She learned just as quickly that she only had to do these things in the class, because at home her owner didn't make her obey the commands. Maggie was certainly an intelligent dog, but trainable? Maggie's owner didn't think so.

What makes a dog trainable? Trainability depends on a combination of personality factors. The average pet owner finds a dependent, passive dog with a low to medium energy level, low reactivity, and passive defense reactions easiest to live with. A dependent personality is probably the most important factor, because it makes a dog anxious to seek your approval. Dogs are harder to train when they are assertive, independent, have a high energy level, or are highly reactive. Nonetheless, any dog without a psychological disorder is trainable. The training techniques described in this book work for dogs of many different personalities. For instance, using food motivates independent dogs that are not motivated by praise as are more dependent dogs. Food rewards help keep the attention of a highly reactive dog, and they reduce the need for force that may induce an assertive dog with active defense reactions to bite.

While training some dogs is easier than others, training is unsuccessful only due to human error, such as failure to communicate what is wanted, failure to adequately motivate, inconsistency, lack of patience, or just plain giving up.

"READING" YOUR DOG

Our dogs speak eloquently to us in a language of their own, a nonverbal language of body and face movements. You need to listen with your eyes to "read" your dog's body language. Understanding this language is essential for two-way communication, and therefore necessary to train your dog and to have a good relationship.

A good way to learn about dog body language is to observe dogs communicating with each other. Give your dog the opportunity to socialize with other dogs, and watch how they interact. How does he greet familiar dogs versus strange dogs? How does he get another dog to play? What games do they play? How do they behave when they get angry at each other?

Another way to learn about your dog's language is to read books on dog and wolf behavior. Since dog and wolf behavior is similar, the interactions of wolves in the wild give scientists a chance to observe communication in a pure form, as it exists without human interference. For example, a dog behavior that many people find annoying is licking people's faces, especially their mouths. The origin of the behavior is rarely seen in dogs, but observations of wolves have shown that wolf puppies are fed by food that is regurgitated by older wolves. This regurgitation is triggered by the wolf pups jumping up and licking at the older wolves' mouths. In this way, wolves could bring home meat from their kills and have it already predigested for their puppies—wolf baby food. This is rarely observed in dogs because puppies are removed from their mothers shortly after weaning. The licking at mouths persists as a greeting behavior in wolves after they have matured. This is why your dog greets you by jumping up and trying to lick your mouth.

Mistakes in interpreting dog body language result in training errors. A common scenario of miscommunication takes place when an owner returns home to find that his dog has destroyed something in his absence. The owner acts angry, and his dog reacts by slinking with his eyes averted or by rolling over onto his side. The owner interprets this behavior to mean that the dog knows what he did wrong and feels guilty. The owner then proceeds to punish him. However, dogs instinctively react to threatening or angry behavior by acting submissively. For instance, my Greyhound acts submissively anytime I am mad, even if it is because I burned dinner or the car broke down. She certainly doesn't know why I am angry. In the case above, the dog is being punished without having the vaguest idea why. He may have committed the destruction minutes after his owner left, and is being punished eight hours later. This punishment will only serve to make him more anxious about his owner coming and going and more likely to react to this stress by destroying something the next time his owner leaves.

As a dog obedience instructor, I often find myself telling a student, "Your dog doesn't understand what you want." This is said to caution a student who is preparing to punish a dog for disobeying a command that the dog doesn't understand in the first place. Typically the disobedience is blamed on the dog's stubbornness. This is another example of how a training error can be committed by misreading a dog. Being able to tell the difference between when your dog is confused and when he is choosing not to obey is critical to good training. A dog's trust is destroyed when he doesn't know what to do to avoid punishment.

Reading your dog is an art. Your dog is already very good at reading you and understanding your emotions by observing your body language. He does it so well that at times he almost seems to read your mind. You owe it to your dog to try to become equally adept at reading him. Developing a friendship with your dog depends on it.

One of the outstanding characteristics of wolf and dog social behavior is their friendliness toward each other.

THE ISSUE OF DOMINANCE

Many dog trainers believe that you must dominate your dog in order to successfully live with him. Obedience training classes ring with the cry, "You must dominate your dog!" and "You must be the pack leader, the alpha figure," a sentiment echoed in many dog training books. It is also claimed that if you don't dominate your dog, he will try to dominate you. Your dog is the enemy; obedience class is often the battleground.

I don't agree with this. You don't have to dominate your dog in order to train him and have a good relationship. The justification given for this insistence on dominance is that a dog's human family is a substitute for a dog pack, and that the social organization of dog packs, like wolf packs, is based on a dominance hierarchy. This dominance hierarchy is supposedly maintained by displays of dominance on the part of the pack leader. Therefore, the reasoning goes, human owners should be dominant over their dogs.

There are many problems with this line of reasoning. First of all, the outstanding characteristic of wolf and dog social behavior is the cooperation and friendliness among pack members, not their struggles for dominance. It is questionable whether the social order of wolves or dogs is based on dominance displays by one individual. Another problem is that dog and human combination "packs" are very different from wolf packs. Besides the obvious fact that there are two different species involved with all of the inherent communication difficulties, humans must control their dogs in ways that have no parallel among wolves. This reasoning is simplistic. The interrelationships of wolves in a pack, or dogs and their human owners, are complex and vary with the individual personalities involved.

For cooperative social groups to function, there have to be differences in personalities so dogs, wolves, or people can serve different functions. As we've previously seen, dogs are born with different personality traits. Just like people, some have more leadership qualities and some are content to be followers. It takes both to make a cooperative social group work. These differences mean that not all dogs want to take over the leadership position, any more than it is true that all people want to be leaders.

Rarely do dogs try to dominate their owners. A dog that doesn't do what the owner wants him to do is not necessarily trying to dominate his owner. Our dogs live in a world full of restraints that prevent them from behaving as they would like. It is natural that they will struggle against them. A dog pulling on the leash is not trying to dominate his owner. He simply wants to go faster or to be free, or maybe even enjoys pulling. Only when extreme assertiveness is combined with active defense reactions and no training do dogs behave in a manner that might be described as dominating their owners.

Emphasis on dominance causes many problems in dog-human relationships. Domination can result in avoidance, fear, and suppression of a dog's initiative. It is possible to dominate a dog by suppressing undesirable behaviors with force while still not communicating to the dog what you want. Mutual communication is cut off when an owner fears that his dog is always trying to dominate him and a dog's initiative to communicate is suppressed. Worst of all, establishing dominance is often used as an excuse for using unnecessary force in dog training.

Dog owners will improve their relationships with their dogs by placing emphasis on respect, clear communication, and mutual cooperation, rather than on dominance. The domestication of dogs has given us power over them by virtue of their dependence on us for survival. We must control our dogs for their safety and well-being, but we must be careful not to abuse this power. Instead, we should use this power in a positive way to allow our dogs to live a happy life and to give ourselves the full benefit of our relationship with dogs.

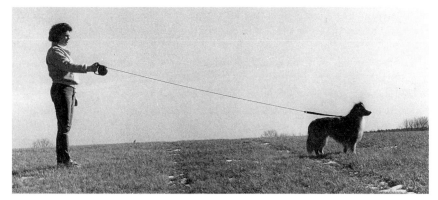

A retractable leash gives your dog the freedom of a longer leash while eliminating the problem of tangling. (Shetland Sheepdog)

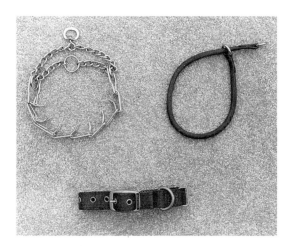

Prong collar, nylon choke collar, buckle collar.

The proper way to put on a choke collar. (Greyhound)

5

Basic Training
the Positive Way

$\mathbf{B}$ASIC TRAINING involves teaching your dog the meaning of commands and motivating your dog to perform them. You will be teaching your dog to sit, stay, come, heel, accept restraint, lie down and stay, not to jump up, and stand and stay. This training can be done with dogs of any age, even an old dog, as long as he is healthy. Puppies should be over ten weeks of age when they start so that they have the necessary physical coordination.

Each command will be taught in several steps, and you can teach more than one command at a time. To help you plan your training, it has been broken down into five weekly assignments, with a test at the end to evaluate your progress. At the beginning of each week's lesson, there will be a list to summarize what you need to practice, followed by a detailed description of how to do it.

You should practice approximately five times a week. How long you should practice depends on your dog. Read your dog to tell when he has had enough. About fifteen minutes is average, but a young puppy may not last that long, while a more exuberant dog may take fifteen minutes just to settle down and begin concentrating. It is better to practice in two shorter sessions per day than one long one. Your dog's concentration span will get longer as training progresses.

Having the right equipment is important for your success in training. You will need a leash, collar, and food treats to train. Let's talk about each of these.

LEASHES

Your leash should be six feet long and made of leather, nylon, or cotton webbing. Do not use a chain leash. Even though your dog won't chew on it the way he might a leather or cotton leash, it will hurt your hands and bang against him. Try to find a leash of appropriate size for your dog. It may be hard to find lightweight leashes with small snaps for Toy dogs. If you have a Toy dog, you may want to try making one yourself. On the other hand, large dogs do not require a leash strong enough to hold a horse. Double layers of nylon tend to be stiff. A large bolt snap could hit your dog in the eye. A ⅝-inch wide leash should be all that is necessary for the largest dog. Cotton web leashes are nice because they soften as you handle them and are inexpensive, a big plus if you are careless about leaving your leash lying around where your dog might chew on it.

A retractable leash is a wonderful invention. While it is not necessary to own one to train your dog, once you own one you'll wonder how you ever got along without it. The retractable leash gives your dog more freedom without the problems of tangling associated with a regular long leash. The leash is encased in a plastic handle that feeds it out when the dog pulls on it and automatically retracts it as the dog returns. It usually comes in sixteen- and twenty-six foot lengths with different strengths suited to dogs of different weights. The handle has a button that stops the leash from extending, acting as a brake.

The retractable leash is wonderful for leash breaking puppies, for teaching a dog to come, and for traveling. Puppies adapt to it more easily than a regular leash because the constant tension is less frightening than suddenly hitting the end of a regular leash and falling over. They don't get tangled up in it. If they grab the leash to play with it, the retractable leash offers no resistance and the puppy loses interest in playing tug-of-war.

The retractable leash is also good for teaching a dog to come. Any of the come exercises described in this chapter can be taught on a retractable leash. The best way to practice with this leash is to allow your dog to wander around, then call him when he is distracted and not paying any attention to you. If he doesn't come, push the brake button and give your dog a jerk to get him moving toward you. When he starts toward you, immediately release the brake button so that the leash can retract as he comes in.

This leash is especially convenient for traveling. It slips easily under the front seat of the car without getting tangled. When you stop or reach your destination, it gives your dog a lot more freedom to exercise safely.

You may also need a long line, which is a leash or rope about thirty feet long, to train your dog to come. This is described in the next chapter.

COLLARS

Dogs need different collars for effective training. You can use a buckle collar, a choke collar, or a prong collar. The choice of collar depends on your dog's size and strength, your size and strength, your dog's pain sensitivity, and his temperament. In my obedience classes for adult dogs, about one third of the dogs are trained on buckle collars, one third are on choke collars, and one third are on prong collars. Of course, obedience classes tend to attract a disproportionate number of large, difficult to control dogs!

Every dog should have a buckle collar, because it is the only collar that is safe to leave on your dog when you are not with him. It is the only collar to use on a puppy under four months of age. Try to do as much of your training as possible on a buckle collar. The collar should be tight enough so that your dog cannot slip out of it. If your dog has a narrow head and there is any chance that your dog may pull out of his buckle collar when he is being walked near traffic, it would be safer to use a choke collar.

If your dog pulls so hard on a buckle collar that your hand and arm hurt, you may have to try something more forceful. The choke collar is the next step up. They can be made of chain or nylon. I prefer the nylon ones because they do not wear off the coat around the neck of a long-haired dog and they slide easier than chain collars. The choke collar should be the smallest size that fits over the dog's head, even if you have to feed your dog's ear through carefully to get it off.

Of the three collars, the choke collar is the most difficult to use properly. If used improperly, it can damage your dog's throat. It has to be put on properly to function as it should. Study the picture showing the right way to put it on, and memorize it. Here are two ways to remember:

1. When your dog is on your left side, the part of the choke collar that you attach your leash to comes *over* the top of your dog's head.
2. Sit your dog in front and facing you. Make a *P* with the collar. Slip it over the dog's head.

Practice putting the collar on several times.

The proper use of the choke collar will be discussed later, in Week 2 of the training plan. Unless you already know how to use one, don't use a choke collar until you have read that discussion. Please don't let your dog pull on his choke collar until he is gasping for air.

If your dog ignores the discomfort of the choke collar, then you might want to try a prong collar. This collar looks like a horrifying instrument of torture, and that is exactly what I thought of it for years before trying it and discovering otherwise. I first used one on a student's dog in desperation. Why two little old ladies had adopted a Saint Bernard cross from the local Humane Society was beyond my understanding, but they did. The first night of obedience classes, my husband had to go out to their car to bring the dog in. I needed to find an easy way for them to control the dog or he most likely faced euthanasia. Finding a home for this monster-sized dog would have been next to impossible. So I tried a prong collar. It worked beautifully. Much to my surprise, the dog did not scream with pain. He learned to walk on a leash.

The typical candidate for a prong collar is a seventy-five-pound male

Labrador Retriever that is totally oblivious to pain, pulls like a maniac, yet has a completely stable personality. How can you tell if your dog needs a prong collar? Ask yourself some questions:

How much does your dog pull?

Are you scared you may be pulled down and hurt when you are walking your dog?

Have you stopped walking your dog because you simply cannot hold him?

Does your dog pull so hard on the leash that he is wheezing and coughing?

How strong are you compared to your dog? Are you a small woman with a big dog?

Do you have arthritis in any part of your arm, a back problem, or are you handicapped?

If your dog is stronger than you are and his pulling has become harmful to you or to him, you need a prong collar.

Pain sensitivity is another factor, an inherited one that tends to run in some breeds more than in others. The puppy testing described in Chapter 3 explains how to test for this trait in a puppy. Pinching the skin between the toes can also give you an idea of an adult dog's pain sensitivity. A dog's reaction to the pressure of a collar is also reduced if he has a thick coat, such as that found on a Chow Chow. As painful as the prong collar looks, most dogs' reaction to it is to scratch at it a little. Dogs simply aren't as pain sensitive as people are.

Your dog's temperament also determines the appropriateness of a prong collar for training. If your dog is easily stressed, nervous, or tends to be aggressive, a prong collar is not for him. The discomfort he may feel may make him too excited. A prong collar is also not a good training tool for someone who loses his temper easily. Be honest with yourself about this for your dog's sake.

Compared to a choke collar, the prong collar is more effective and easier to use. It gives you power steering. The prong collar is safer because it is made in a way that allows it only to be closed a certain amount. The choke collar can close until a dog strangles. Neither collar should be left on your dog when you are not with him. Hopefully, when you have progressed in your training, neither collar will be necessary.

TREATS

You will need food treats every time you train your dog, and lots of them! The treats should be something small, because you don't want to have your dog's hunger run out before you are finished training. They should also be something that your dog doesn't need to chew a lot to swallow. You might try slices of hot dog, semimoist cat treats, or dog treats. Pieces the size of a marble are good for medium and large dogs. One of my students uses Cheerios because her dog is on a special diet. If you like to cook, you might want to try homemade dog treats. For the fussy eater, try pepperoni or cooked beef liver.

Liver is a traditional favorite among professional dog show handlers. To cook the beef liver, boil it in water until the blood color is gone, then bake it in a 300°F oven until it is dried but not crispy. Let it cool and cut it into pieces. The aroma in your house may not be pleasant, but your dog will love it. If he still turns up his nose, try sprinkling the liver with garlic powder before baking it.

If your dog won't eat treats, you are probably overfeeding him, he is terribly stressed, or he has a health problem. You need to solve these problems before beginning training. If your dog is overweight, you should still train with food treats. Just make sure to cut back on the rest of his food.

To keep your food treats quickly accessible, it is helpful to have some sort of small bag or pouch that you can attach to your waist. An easy way to make one is to cut the back pocket off an old pair of jeans, leaving about two inches of material above the pocket. You can then pin this to your waist in front of you with a large safety pin.

BASIC TRAINING SKILLS

First, a word about commands. Commands are word signals. When you train, these word signals are usually accompanied by body motions. Your dog is better at reading body language than understanding separate words because he doesn't naturally communicate with words. Because of this, he will pick up on body signals faster than word signals. That's okay. It is important that you are aware of this so that you are not frustrated when he doesn't respond to the word alone. He will also pay more attention to the inflection you use when you give a command than the individual word. Word signals are hard for dogs to learn because they are not natural for them.

You can help your dog learn these word signals we call commands more easily if you are consistent in your use of them. Just think how you would feel if you were learning a foreign language, and instead of teaching you one word at a time, someone kept giving you five different synonyms for the same thing. Instead of just learning "friend," one day you heard "friend," and the next day "comrade," and the next day "companion," "buddy," and "chum." This is how your dog feels when he hears "come," "come here," "here," and "get over here." So stick to one word and use it consistently. Make sure everyone in your family uses the same words, too.

When you give a command involving movement, it is usually best to say your dog's name first, to get his attention, and then give him the word signal, or command. Realize that this is the opposite of how we normally talk. We usually say, "How are you, John?" We put the person's name at the *end* of the sentence. Be conscious of this so that you are careful to always say your dog's name before the appropriate command, not after. Give your commands in a friendly but firm tone of voice. There's no need to be loud, either. If your dog can hear the sound of a box of dog treats being opened when he is three rooms away, he can hear you speaking in a normal tone of voice.

This dog is showing signs of stress. Reading your dog's body language is important for successful training.

The order in which you give praise and food treats is important, too. In Chapter 1, under "Other Rewards," it was explained that by giving the praise *before* the food treat, the praise becomes a conditioned reward. Remember, too, that praise is important as reassurance for your dog. Read this section in Chapter 1 again before beginning training. Also remember that praise, such as "good dog," is used differently from the release word "okay." If you need to review this idea, see Chapter 3 under "Teaching Commands: Sit, Stay, Okay, and No."

Whenever you are teaching your dog a new command, the training should be done in a place where your dog (and you) won't be distracted. Whenever possible, start the training indoors. Make sure you are the only person in the room. Once your dog is responding well, gradually add distractions and try the same exercise outdoors. Your goal is to have your dog respond to commands anywhere and under any conditions. You will have to practice in many places and with all the distractions of everyday life to achieve this.

A part of reading your dog that will improve your training is being able to anticipate when your dog is going to make a mistake, and preventing it from happening. For example, when your dog is on a sit-stay, you want to correct him when he thinks about getting up, not after he has already gotten up and walked a few steps away. Your dog will give you signs that he is about to get up. He might get restless and make small movements, like picking up a paw. He might look around. Then, right before he gets up, he has to shift his weight forward. This is the time to caution him to stay, saying "No, stay" in a firm tone of voice. You have to pay close attention to your dog to read him in a situation like this.

TEN RULES FOR GOOD TRAINING

1. If you are in a bad mood or irritated at someone, don't train your dog. It will be too tempting to take it out on your dog.
2. If your dog is too full of energy to concentrate, exercise him before training.
3. Make sure your dog is hungry when you start training.
4. If you feel yourself losing your temper, stop training.
5. Read your dog carefully so you know when he is becoming stressed. Signs of stress might be looking away from you, partially closing his eyes, a droopy tail, lips pressed tightly together, and trying to get away from you. If you see these signs, back up and make the exercise easier.
6. If you are having trouble with one part of the training, move on to something else and come back to the trouble spot later.
7. Be more stubborn than your dog is.
8. Be 100 percent sure that your dog understands what you want before assuming he is choosing not to obey you.

9. You must pay as much attention to your dog as you expect him to pay to you.
10. Always end your practice session by playing with your dog for a few minutes.

Go get your dog and let's get started!

LESSON PLANS

Week 1

Review the sit and sit-stay for food
Sitting on command without food in your hand
Sit-stay in heel position for thirty seconds
Sit-stay in heel position with distractions
Sit-stay for petting
Sit-stay with eye contact
Come and sit with food

Review the sit and sit-stay for food

This is described in Chapter 3 under "Teaching Commands: Sit, Stay, Okay, and No."

Sitting on command without food in your hand

This is a simple but important exercise. Previously, you have always had a piece of food in your hand when you asked your dog to sit. Now you are going to ask your dog to sit without having the food in your hand, although you will still use food as a reward. To understand the significance of this step, you need to understand the difference between a lure and a reward. When food is used as a lure, it is shown to the dog *before* the dog responds. When food is used as a reward, it is not shown to the dog until *after* the dog responds.

You may have trouble making the transition between using the food as a lure and a reward because your dog may not respond at first if he thinks the food is unavailable. Be patient. The first time you ask your dog to sit without the food in your hand, make the exact same hand motion as you did when you had food. This then becomes your sit hand signal. When your dog sits, reach into your pocket or a nearby container to reward your dog with a piece of food.

Sit-stay in heel position for thirty seconds

Sit your dog in heel position, which is a convenient and traditional way of referring to placing your dog on your left side so he is facing in the same direction you are, with his head lined up approximately with your left leg. Have your dog on leash. To get him in this position, you may either lure him into position with a piece of food, or you may position him with your hands. To physically position him, put your right hand on his collar and your left hand on his rump near the base of his tail. Pull up and back with your right hand, and push down with your left hand. Be careful not to push in the middle of his back. Give the command to sit ("Max, sit") as you do so. Now is a good time to get into the habit of making your dog respond to the first command. If you never make your dog sit until you have given the command several times, increasing the loudness of your voice with each command, then he will always wait for that.

Praise and reward him with a small food treat for sitting. Remember the importance of that order. He should not get up when you praise, only when he is given the "okay" release word. If he does get up, say "No, sit," sit him again, and resume praising him.

Once he is sitting, tell him to stay. You may want to omit saying his name before the stay command, because some dogs will want to get up when they hear their name. On the other hand, if you've lost his attention, you may want to say his name first. At the same time that you give him a command to stay, bring your right hand across your body to stop just in front of your dog's nose, palm facing toward him.

Start with whatever amount of time is easy for him to stay, maybe ten seconds. Hold a piece of food in your hand to help keep his attention. If he absolutely will not hold still for a few seconds, go back to the sit-stay for food until he will stay in position for a few seconds without being held there physically. When he stays for whatever length of time you set as your goal, praise, reward with a treat, and release him with "Okay!"

Your goal is to have him sit for thirty seconds on a loose leash. Build up to that time gradually.

Sit-stay in heel position with distractions

When you ask your dog to sit and stay in everyday life, he won't always be in a quiet room by himself. You want to teach him to stay in distracting circumstances.

Start again with your dog sitting in heel position, on your left side, on leash. Don't forget to reward or at least praise him for sitting. Tell him to stay as you give him the stay hand signal. Then bring on the distractions. Start with ones that are not difficult for your dog to resist, then build up to the harder ones. Distractions can be as simple as someone walking in a circle around you and your dog. Harder ones are someone running by, riding a bicycle by, or throwing a ball past you. This is the time to teach your dog to control his instinct to chase things, which often leads dogs into streets where they are killed. A challenging distraction in our classes is Mr. Spider, a windup cat toy that bounces and spins wildly across the room. If you have children, challenge them to come up with distrac-

Eye contact is a special way to communicate with your dog. (Golden Retriever)

tions. The rules are that they can do anything they want, except call your dog's name.

If your dog continually gets up, keep sitting him again and again until he stays. There is no need to use more force; just be more stubborn than he is. If you initially have to hold him in place, do it. When he does stay, praise, reward, and release.

Sit-stay for petting

Do you have problems with your dog jumping up? This is the problem people list most often on the registration form for my classes. Here is how you start solving that problem.

Doing a sit-stay for petting is just like doing any other sit-stay with distractions. Again, start with your dog sitting in heel position, then have someone approach and pet him while you keep him sitting. Start with someone familiar to your dog, so he will be less excited. If he can't remain sitting while someone is approaching, don't let them pet him until he can do it. Your helper may have to approach your dog several times until he settles down and stays. Keep at it until he relaxes. The next time you practice, it should take fewer approaches to get him to stay. Don't forget to make him stay until you release him with "Okay."

Sit-stay with eye contact

It is impossible to communicate with your dog, or with another person for that matter, unless you have his attention. Teaching your dog to make eye contact is teaching your dog to look at you when you are speaking to him, a necessary foundation for all training.

Start by sitting your dog in front of you, facing you, and tell him to stay. Take a piece of food and move it slowly from in front of your dog's nose up to the bridge of your nose, between your eyes. As you are moving the food, give your dog a command ("Max, watch"). If your dog breaks his sit-stay or jumps up to grab the food, sit him again and start over. When your dog makes eye contact, praise him quietly, give him the food you had been holding up to your eyes, and release.

When your dog has caught on to the idea, ask him to watch for gradually increasing lengths of time. Start by asking him to watch while you silently count to five. If your dog looks away and breaks eye contact, move the food back to his nose to get his attention and start over. Don't ask for more than ten seconds this week.

It has been said that the eyes are the window to the soul. Nowhere is this more true than with dogs. Dogs say so much with their eyes. There is more to this exercise than just getting your dog's attention. It is a special way to make contact with your dog. Not only are you getting your dog's attention, you are also giving him yours. It is a mutual sharing. Whenever you are with your dog,

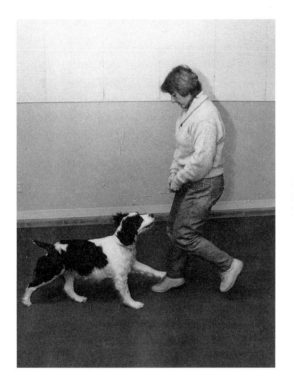

Back away from your dog, using the food as a magnet to keep your dog in front of you.

After a few steps, stop and bring the food up to signal your dog to sit as you give the sit command.   (English Springer Spaniel)

try to make eye contact. When you do, smile at him. That is an easy way to express love.

Come and sit with food

The purpose of this exercise is to teach your dog the meaning of the word "come." It is the first of many steps in teaching your dog to come. The reason you are teaching your dog to sit in front of you is so that you can easily reach down and restrain him. Many people lunge and grab their dogs when they get close, inadvertently teaching their dogs to play keep away. Have you ever seen an owner and dog playing this game? The owner stands very still, hardly breathing, waiting for his dog to come close enough to be grabbed. When the dog gets close enough, the owner lunges. Since dogs have a well-developed ability to perceive movement, they see the grab coming and dart away. Then the game starts over, with the owner waiting frustrating amounts of time for their dog to come close again. Teaching your dog to come and sit can prevent this.

Begin teaching this exercise indoors. Start with your dog sitting in front of you. Since he is inside, he doesn't need to be on leash. Hold both your hands in front of you with a piece of food in them, at your dog's nose level. Give your dog a command to come in an inviting tone of voice. Back up quickly about four steps. Backing away takes advantage of your dog's instinct to chase. Use the food as a magnet to keep your dog in front of you. As you stop, bring the food up to signal your dog to sit and give the sit command. You should give the sit command and signal a moment before you stop so that your dog has time to slow down. Praise, reward, and release. Do *not* touch your dog to get him to sit. You will know he is getting the idea when he sits automatically without your having to tell him.

Once your dog is doing this well in the house, try it outdoors. Of course, have your dog on leash if you are in an unfenced area, but try to keep the leash loose. Don't use it to guide the dog in any way. You want the food, not the leash, to control your dog.

Week 2

Sit-stay at the end of the leash
Sit-stay away from home
Eye contact without food in your hands
Come and take hold of the collar
Come with food from a distance
Heeling
Downing on command
Restraint

Sit-stay at the end of the leash

Teaching your dog to sit and stay when you are a leash-length away from him is the first step in teaching him to stay while you move about. Having him on leash makes it easier for you to quickly reposition him if he moves. Start with him sitting in heel position. Did you remember to reward him for sitting? Give him the stay command and hand signal.

Slowly back away to the end of the leash. You can repeat the hand signal and stay command as necessary. If you repeat the command, you may want to omit his name, so he isn't confused and doesn't think you want him to come to you. Be careful not to pull him with the leash by mistake and cause him to move. Read him carefully so you can anticipate any moves and remind him to stay. If he moves, put him back into the place he was originally, and start over.

After you have reached the end of the leash, immediately return to him. Go all the way back to heel position, where you started. Do *not* call him to you. Calling him out of a stay will confuse him at this point. He will anticipate your call and will keep getting up to come to you. Make him stay until you are all the way back in heel position, and then praise, reward, and release. Gradually increase the amount of time he will stay at the end of the leash to one minute. It will probably take two weeks to get up to one minute.

Sit-stay away from home

By now your dog should be doing the sit-stay in heel position at home very reliably. You are probably still working on steadiness with distractions. Now you want to teach your dog that he has to listen to your commands away from home, too. When you are working away from home, start with things he knows well. It is normal to have to backtrack a little. Take him with you when you run an errand, like a trip to the post office, and just quickly get him out of the car and make him do a sit-stay in heel position. Try to find a place away from home, both indoors and outdoors, where you can practice this. Do you have an understanding friend or relative who wouldn't mind if you practiced inside their home? Don't forget to bring your treats to reward him and help keep his attention in a distracting situation.

Eye contact without food in your hands

Just as when teaching your dog to sit on command without food in your hand, this exercise makes the same transition from using the food as a lure to using the food as a reward. First, warm up by doing the eye contact exercise as you practiced it last week, with the food in your hands. After one or two repetitions, bring the index finger of your right hand up to the corner of your right eye, without food in either hand, and tell your dog to watch (''Max, watch''). If he makes eye contact, praise him and reward him with a treat. If you're having difficulty, try touching him on his nose or the side of his face to get his attention, and then bringing your finger up to your eye. Be patient as you make this transition, and be quick to reward even a glance.

Come and take hold of the collar

This exercise is the same as the come and sit exercise from last week, except this time when your dog sits you are going to reach down and take hold of his collar before you praise and reward him. You want to make sure he is comfortable with this motion and that he won't jump away. Have the food in your right hand, so that your left hand is free to take hold of the collar. Give your dog the food while you are still holding on to the collar. Remember, the sequence is:

1. "Max, come," as you back away.
2. "Max, sit," as you stop.
3. Take hold of the collar.
4. Praise.
5. Reward.
6. Release with "Okay."

As your dog becomes more comfortable with this, you may want to reach and grab faster, as you might in an emergency, to accustom him to this. You should also practice calling your dog to you and snapping on the leash before praising him and giving him his reward.

Come with food from a distance

Until now when you practiced the come and sit, your dog has been in front of you. Now you want to add some distance. There are several ways to do this. One is to call your dog to you when he is in another room. Make sure you have a treat available at least three quarters of the time to reward him.

Another way to practice this is to have someone hold your dog while you go five to ten feet away and call him. Give him the sit command before he gets to you so that he has time to slow down. The idea is *not* to have your dog run at you full speed, crash into you, and then sit down. Gradually increase the distance between you and your helper.

A good way to practice this if you have other people in your household is to call the dog from one person to another. If there are three people, they can form a triangle to practice. For your dog's own safety, he should respond to a come command from any member of your family. Everyone's command will sound different to him because of different voices, so he has to get used to all of them. Even children as young as three or four years old can participate in this ·exercise. This is a fun game for everyone. Once your dog gets the idea, he will start to race to the next person without a command! It's a great way to exercise a dog.

Heeling

Heeling can refer to two different things: the highly stylized precision heeling of the obedience show ring, and being able to comfortably walk your dog

Teach your dog to walk slowly by keeping him on a short leash.

Use food as a magnet to keep your dog in heel position. (German Shepherd)

on leash. It is the latter that you will be learning, although if you want to go on to obedience competition, you will have a good foundation for show heeling with this method of training. This training assumes that your dog is somewhat accustomed to walking on a leash.

When your dog heels, he should walk on your left side (the left side is traditional) without pulling on the leash. This is not natural for a dog to do and is difficult for your dog to learn. The instructions for you to follow will be fairly complicated, too, so be prepared to be patient with both your dog and yourself. This week you will be working on the three different parts of teaching heeling, practicing them separately. Next week you will combine them. The following week you will try heeling in more distracting circumstances. This week work in the most distraction-free area you can find. You will both need to concentrate!

PART 1: TEACHING YOUR DOG TO WALK SLOWLY

Dogs pull on their leashes because they want to go faster than we do, so we have to teach them to accept walking at a slower pace. You are going to do that by exaggerating and walking slower than usual.

Start by sitting your dog in heel position. Hold your right hand by your left hip. While you hold your leash in that position, gather it up so that the leash forms a straight line between your right hand and your dog. Put your left hand on the leash below your right hand. Don't hold it so tight that you are pulling the collar tight. Give your dog a command to heel ("Max, heel"), and start walking very slowly. Your goal is to keep his ear right by your left leg. Do this for about ten steps at first.

As you stop, release your dog with an "Okay" command. In the show ring, your dog is required to sit when you stop. However, this is unnecessary and inconvenient when you are walking your dog for exercise.

When your dog does this with little resistance, gradually extend the distance. Remember to keep walking slowly.

PART 2: HEELING WITH FOOD

In order for your dog not to pull, he has to pay attention to where he is in relation to you, so he has to watch you. Using food is a good way to encourage him to do this. The food will show your dog in a positive way where you want him to be.

Gather up the leash in a straight line between you and your dog, this time in your left hand. Have about five pieces of food in your right hand. Hold your right hand close to your dog's nose. When the dog's attention is focused on your right hand, give him the command to heel and start walking forward slowly. Every two to three steps, give him a piece of food. Try to keep walking as you do it. This will be difficult at first, but you'll get better at getting it in your dog's mouth, and he'll learn to eat while he's walking. When your food runs out, release him.

The food in your right hand should act like a magnet to hold your dog in position. Try to let the food control him so that the leash never gets tight. If he is jumping up at your hands, you are holding the food too far away from his nose. If you have to hold him back with the leash to keep him by your leg, you are holding the food too far in front of you. And if he isn't interested in the food you have, get something he likes better!

PART 3: THE CORRECTION

When your dog pulls on the leash, you need a way to stop him. This is done with a jerk on the leash that is traditionally called a "correction." It is a mild form of force that is used to get a dog's attention, and can be used in many different situations.

To give a correction, you must put some slack in the leash, then suddenly jerk the collar in a rapid, snapping movement, followed by an immediate release of tension or pressure on the collar. This is not an easy thing to learn how to do. The purpose of the correction is to get your dog's attention, not to move him from one place to another. It should briefly knock your dog off balance and cause him to stop whatever he was doing and look at you.

Before you try it on your dog, practice on someone's arm. Have them stand on your left side and hold their right arm out at a ninety-degree angle from their body. Pretend their arm is your dog's neck. Put a buckle or choke collar on their arm with the leash attached. Instruct them to try to hold their arm as still as possible. Then try giving them a correction. You will find that if you gradually apply pressure to the leash, they will be able to resist. However, if you make a quick snap, their arm will move.

Once you have the idea, try it on your dog. Start with your dog sitting in heel position. Hold your leash as in Part 1, but allow a little slack in the leash. Then give him the heel command and start walking slowly. When your dog starts pulling on the leash, stop walking and then jerk the leash with your left hand across your body. Tell your dog, "No, don't pull" as you give the correction. The jerk should be just hard enough to get your dog's attention and no harder. Don't start walking again until you have your dog's attention and he has stopped pulling. Be persistent, even if it means stopping every other step. Don't let your dog get more than a few inches in front of you before correcting him. Use praise to reassure your dog immediately following a correction so he is not frightened of you.

If you have to pull so hard to get your dog's attention that the front half of his body is moved, try a more forceful collar. It is less harmful for your dog's neck to get a more effective collar than to increase the strength of the jerk.

Practice each of these parts separately. Do Part 1 for ten to fifteen steps, Part 2 for another ten to fifteen steps, Part 3 for ten to fifteen steps, and then repeat all three parts over again. Keep talking to your dog to keep his attention and to reassure him.

A leash correction should surprise your dog and get his attention.

Downing on command

Good news. Heeling is generally hard to teach your dog, but teaching your dog to lie down on command is fairly easy. Sit your dog on your left side, and kneel beside him. Do this indoors, so your dog won't need to be on leash. Place your left hand lightly on your dog's rump so that he cannot stand up. Have a piece of food in your right hand. Hold the food near your dog's nose and use it like a magnet to draw your dog to the floor. At the same time that you do this, give your dog a command to down ("Max, down"). Your dog may not be able to figure out what to do at first. If he needs help, use your left hand to push down on your dog's shoulders to encourage him to lie down. As soon as his elbows touch the floor, pop the food into his mouth. Don't try to get him to stay down at this point. You only want to teach him to lie down on command.

Restraint

The importance of a dog accepting restraint was discussed in Chapter 3 under "Teaching Commands: Sit, Stay, Okay, and No." This exercise will further develop your dog's ability to accept restraint, this time in a lying down position.

Sit your dog in heel position, and kneel beside him. Then make him lie down. It doesn't matter how you do it. You can use food to down him as described in the above exercise. You can also physically put him in a down position. To do this, put your left arm over his back and grasp his left front leg. Hold his right front leg with your right hand. Slowly slide his legs forward until his elbows are on the ground.

Once your dog is down, gently roll him over onto his side. Press his head down flat against the floor. Tell him to stay and repeat the command as necessary. Hold him there with one hand on his neck and one on his hindquarters. When he relaxes, you can just quietly pet him as he lies there. Gradually work up to having your dog stay in this position for one minute. Release him with an "Okay" and give him a reward. This is easy to practice while you are watching TV.

Some dogs may strenuously resist doing this. It is important to be more stubborn than he is. He may even be frightened. If he is, it is important for him to learn that he will not be hurt, so don't give up. If your dog struggles strongly, it may be helpful to try a different position. Kneel so that your dog's back is against your knees and his legs are facing away from you when he is on his side. Hold the front and back legs that are closest to the ground. Hold your dog in this position until he relaxes. When he does, praise him quietly, release, and reward.

If at any point in doing this you think your dog might bite you, stop immediately and seek the help of an experienced dog trainer.

Week 3

Sit-stay off leash
Sit-stay with owner moving

Use food as a magnet to pull your dog into a down position.

Teaching your dog to accept restraint can prevent aggressive behavior when your dog is groomed, examined by a veterinarian, or hugged by a child. (English Springer Spaniel)

Eye contact, no hand signal
Heeling: Combining the parts
Come away from distractions
Downing without food in hand
Down-stay

Sit-stay off leash

You do not want your dog to think that he only has to be obedient when he is on leash. This week practice your sit-stay indoors off leash. Start with having your dog do an off-leash sit-stay at your side for fifteen to thirty seconds. Then try leaving him and going about six to ten feet away, again off leash. Remember to return to him and make him wait until you give him the "Okay" release. Next try some off-leash sit-stays with your dog in heel position with some mild distractions. Finally, try an off-leash sit-stay with someone approaching and petting your dog. Praise, reward, and release as usual.

Sit-stay with owner moving

For your sit-stay training to be useful, your dog has to be able to stay while you move around. Start this with your dog on leash. Having your dog on leash will make it easier for you to reposition him. Many dogs will think they can move when you move, so be patient.

The first time you try it, go to the end of the leash and walk back and forth in front of your dog. If he stays, return to him, praise, reward, and release. If he gets up, keep putting him back into a sitting position until he gets the idea. Repeat the stay command as necessary. Once he can do this well, try dropping the leash and walking in a circle around him. For a real challenge, try doing jumping jacks or running in place in front of him. Once he can perform a reliable sit-stay on leash, repeat the process off leash.

Eye contact, no hand signal

This exercise has two purposes: (1) To teach your dog to look at you with a verbal command only and no hand signal; and (2) to further educate you and your dog in the use of food as a reward rather than as a lure. When you finish teaching your dog this exercise, you should have a better understanding of how positive reinforcement works. This is hard for your dog to understand, so practice in a quiet area initially.

First, warm up with last week's eye contact exercise by telling your dog to watch, then pointing to your eyes, without food in your hands. When he makes eye contact, praise, reward, and release.

When you are successful at that, try telling him to watch while your hands are hanging at your sides. There should be no food in them. If he looks up and makes eye contact, reward him with a piece of food. If he doesn't, keep talking to him softly or make kissing noises. The second he looks up, immediately stuff food in his mouth. Once he understands what you want, try to extend the amount of time he holds eye contact before you reward him. Don't ask him to hold it for longer than a count of five.

Heeling: Combining the parts

This week you are going to combine all three parts of heeling as you practice, still in a quiet area. This means slowing your dog down, giving food rewards, and making corrections for pulling. For a while it will feel like you are trying to rub your stomach and pat your head at the same time.

Start by reviewing Part 2, heeling with food, so that your dog is motivated. Then, with your dog sitting in heel position, hold the leash as you did in Part 3 last week. Have your food treats handy. Give the heel command, and start off slowly. Concentrate on keeping your dog walking slowly with his ear by your left leg. Correct for pulling as necessary. Keep his attention by talking to him. If he walks for a few steps without pulling, stop, transfer the entire leash to your left hand, and give him a reward. Don't release him so you can continue heeling without starting all over. After about ten to fifteen steps, release him. Try to keep the leash loose as much as possible.

When your dog is heeling well slowly, gradually increase the speed until you reach normal walking speed. Every time he gets out of control, go back to working at slow speed. You should begin to be able to give the pulling corrections without stopping. If your dog starts to pull, warn him ("Max, don't pull"), and wait to see if he will respond by backing off before giving him a correction.

Come away from distractions

Distractions are the main reason that dogs do not come when called. If your dog doesn't come away from distractions when he is on leash, it is obviously unlikely that he will do so when off leash. To practice this, you may have to set up some distractions ahead of time. You want to litter your yard or practice area with things that will distract your dog. Good things might be a closed plastic container with food in it, or an unopened package of dog treats. When things are set up, go get your dog and put him on leash. Have a treat handy to reward him, but don't let him see it, otherwise he may not want to leave you. Let him wander around until he spots the distraction. Follow him around and keep the leash loose. When he is busy investigating, call him ("Max, come"). If he doesn't come, give the leash a quick tug, back up a few steps as you did when you were initially teaching him to come, and guide him into a sit as you stop. Even though he didn't come on his own, you should still praise and reward him for coming. Start to praise him the second he turns away from the distraction and comes toward you. Do not drag him all the way to you on a tight leash; just give him a tug to get him started. It is okay if he picks up the distracting article and brings it to you.

If your dog does come when you call him, reward him. Then plan a more challenging distraction.

You can practice this anytime you walk your dog. If he is sniffing the place where every neighborhood dog lifts his leg, or if he is straining at the end of the leash toward the neighbor's cat, call him, give him a tug, and back up.

Downing without food in hand

Downing your dog without food in hand is another transition from lure to reward. By making this transition, your dog won't be dependent on food for obeying.

Warm him up by asking him to down a few times with food in your hand. Remember, we are not asking him to stay at this point. When he is downing well with the food, try one without. Simply make the exact same hand movement you made when you had food. Don't forget to give a verbal command at the same time. It may be necessary to repeat the command and hand signal. When your dog lies down, reward him with a treat and praise. Be patient but persistent.

Down-stay

The down-stay is one of the most useful commands you can teach your dog. You already have prepared for it by working on downing your dog and the restraint exercise. Practice the down-stay indoors. You shouldn't have to set aside a special time to do this. Anytime you are sitting down, perhaps watching TV or reading, is fine. Start this training in a quiet, nondistracting situation to encourage your dog to relax.

Start by downing your dog with a piece of food. When he is down, tell him to stay *before* you give him the piece of food. He may want to pop up when he gets the food, because up until now this was the end of the exercise. Try to anticipate him getting up. If he does, put him back down by pulling his feet out, as described in the Restraint exercise in Week 2. Repeat the stay command as necessary. Sit on the ground beside your dog, petting him if that helps him relax. Go for one minute the first time.

When he is good at this, try doing a down-stay while you are sitting in a chair with him at your feet. Gradually increase the time to five minutes.

Week 4

Stay in car and at door
Eye contact, looking away from food
Stand
Off
Heeling: Going for a walk
Down-stay with distractions
Sit-stay for ear cleaning and teeth exam

Handling paws on down-stay
Come from sit-stay

Stay in car and at door

For any of this training to be useful, it has to be incorporated into your everyday life with your dog. Using the sit-stay when you get out of the car and at doors in your house are examples of training exercises becoming an integral part of your life. Training exercises isolate what you are trying to teach your dog in situations where you and your dog can concentrate.

These stay exercises are important in protecting your dog's life. Dogs that bolt through doors, be they car doors or house doors, are endangering their lives. The time to teach your dog to stay at doors is not when you are in a hurry to go somewhere, but when you can concentrate on training your dog.

Your dog should stay while you get out of the car, open the back door, attach a leash to his collar, and give him the "Okay" command. It may be helpful when you first try this to have his leash already attached to his collar. He does not need to sit first, but if you think that will help, go ahead and make him sit. Tell him to stay before you open your car door. If he leaps into the front seat and tramples you in an attempt to exit, close the door before he can escape, somehow get him into the back seat, and start over. Be stubborn. If he leaps out the back door before you give him the "Okay," put him back in the car and make him do a sit-stay with the car door open.

You should also be able to tell your dog to stay and then open any door in the house without having him bolt through. Make it easy at first by doing this when your dog has just been exercised and is tired. You can do this on leash, placing your dog in a sit-stay a few feet from the door. Open the door slowly. If your dog gets up, slam the door shut, put him back in a sit, and start over. Be sure to have the treats ready to reward him when he gets it right.

Once your dog is doing this well, attempt it when someone is outside knocking on the door. This will be a real challenge, but wouldn't it be great if your dog behaved in a somewhat civilized manner when people came to the house?

Have a family member or friend help you—someone who won't mind knocking on the door several times and having the door slammed in his face. When your helper knocks, follow your dog to the door, put his leash on, and tell him to sit and stay. This alone may be a challenge, so don't progress any further until you get this part under control. Then open the door. As before, if your dog moves, shut the door without allowing your helper to enter, and start over. Your goal is to have your dog stay while you open the door, the helper enters, you shut the door, and you say "Okay." Have you helper come and go several times in a practice session, so that your dog gets used to it, is less excited, and has more chance of being successful. Put this training to use whenever someone comes to your house. Have your dog on leash before you open the door.

Teaching a dog to stay when you open a door can save his life. (Shetland Sheepdog)

Eye contact, looking away from food

When you are using food to train your dog, it is helpful to teach your dog that he should look at you and pay attention to you, not the food. Sit your dog in front of you, as in previous eye contact exercises. Have a piece of food in each hand, closed in a fist. Hold your fists at your sides. Your dog should know you have food in your hands. Give him a watch command. More than likely, he will stare at your hands and nudge at them with his nose. Ignore this. Keep giving him the watch command, softly calling his name or making funny noises. Hopefully, he will eventually glance at your face. When he does, give him one of the pieces of food in your hands. Repeat until he instantly looks at you and away from the food when he hears his name.

Stand

As I was writing this chapter, I decided I needed a break and took my dogs for a short walk in the woods behind my house. (Actually, it was my dogs who decided I needed a break.) They started a major excavation project in search of a chipmunk that had gone underground. When I ended their game, they were both covered with mud. We all returned home, and I was faced with the problem of muddy feet and light beige carpets. Obedience training to the rescue! I told the dogs to stand and stay while I dunked their feet in a bucket of water and then wiped them off.

The stand-stay is useful in many ways: for veterinary examinations, for grooming, as part of learning not to jump up, and, of course, for wiping muddy feet. Start by sitting your dog in heel position. If you have a small or medium-sized dog, kneel beside him. If your dog is on leash, put the leash under your knee or your foot, so that both hands are free. Take a piece of food in your right hand. Hold it close to your dog's nose. Give him a command to stand ("Max, stand") as you move your hand away from his nose and parallel to the ground. With a big dog, you may have to take a step forward. Encourage him to stand up by slipping your left hand under his belly and lifting him to his feet. As soon as he stands up, give him the food, release him ("Okay"), and praise. Do not try to make him stay at first.

There is another method for getting your dog in a standing position when you don't have food. Start in the same position, with your dog on your left side, kneeling if necessary. With your right hand, grasp your dog's collar under his chin. As you give your command to stand, pull your dog forward into a standing position. As with the above method, use your left hand under his belly to encourage him to stand.

The most common error people make in training their dogs to stand is to pull up on the collar in a motion similar to the one used to sit a dog, so the dog is confused. Be careful not to do this. The difference is that to sit a dog you hold the collar on top of the dog's neck, and pull up and back. To stand a dog you hold the collar underneath the chin, and pull parallel to the ground.

Teaching your dog to stand stay will make it easier for your veterinarian to examine him.　(German Shorthaired Pointer)

Off

The command "Off" means *don't touch.* You will use it to warn your dog not to jump up on you or other people. Start by showing your dog a piece of food and encouraging him to jump up to get it. Then tell him "Max, off." Your tone of voice should be firm enough to stop him, but if it isn't, push your dog down. The minute he gets all four paws on the ground, reward him with the piece of food. Show him another piece of food. This time warn him with "Off" before he starts to jump. If he restrains himself, reward him.

Once he gets the idea of not jumping up on you, practice with someone else. Have a helper hold a piece of food. You should have your dog on leash for easier restraint. As your dog starts to jump at the food, say "Off." You give the command, as opposed to the helper giving the command, because you want to be able to use this word to stop your dog from jumping up on anyone. Use the leash to restrain your dog as necessary. Have your helper talk to your dog in the high-pitched, excited tone of voice most people use to greet a dog. Again, warn him with his off command, and reward him if he doesn't jump up.

This command can also be used to warn a dog not to jump up to get food on a counter or to touch something like a plate of food sitting on a coffee table. You can also use it to get your dog off the furniture.

Many people use the word "down" to discourage a dog that is jumping up. Don't make this mistake. First of all, we are already using that word to mean something else: for the dog to lie down. Second, you will tend not to use "down" as a warning word to prevent your dog from jumping up. The goal is not to have a word to stop your dog from jumping up once he is doing it, but to give your dog a warning to prevent him from doing it in the first place. This way he can develop good habits and be rewarded for them, not punished for greeting a person in a way that is natural for him.

Heeling: Going for a walk

It is time to take your heeling act on the road and try out your heeling skills as you go for a walk. Your dog will probably be very excited at the start of your walk and pull like crazy. Be realistic about your expectations. If this is the highlight of his day, be tolerant of a little exuberance at the beginning of the walk. Also, make allowances before setting out for the call of nature. However, no matter how excited he is, do not give him all six feet of the leash and let him drag you down the street. Just let him bounce around for a minute, maybe on a retractable leash or long line, before beginning your walk. Then start by telling him to sit to get him under control. Give a heel command, and take off. Keep the leash fairly snug. Make him walk at your speed, not his. If you have to stop and correct twenty-five times before you even reach the end of the driveway, do so. He will improve, but only if you practice. Don't get discouraged and give up. And don't forget to bring your treats along to reward him and to help keep his attention. Give him treats frequently. If you find yourself having to repeatedly

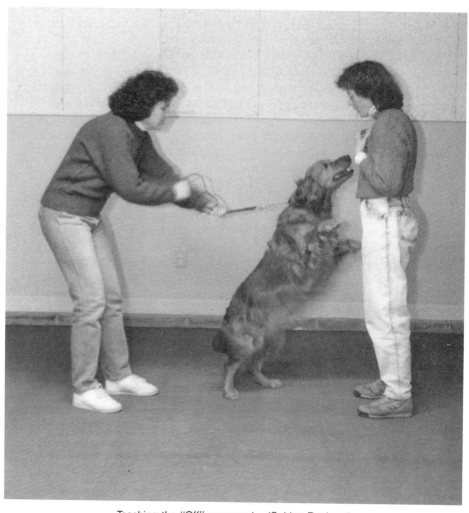

Teaching the "Off" command. (Golden Retriever)

give him corrections for pulling, you should consider trying a more effective collar.

Once you start walking, don't let him stop to sniff or wander around. Both of you will only get the aerobic benefits of walking if you don't stop (except, of course, to make a correction)!

Make up your mind that you are never again going to let your dog pull you when you go for a walk. *Never.* This is the only way that you will break his habit of pulling.

Down-stay with distractions

This week practice your down-stay with distractions. These could be the kids running around the living room or you getting up and walking around. If your dog begs for food, even if that only means staring at you and pleading with his eyes, put him on a down-stay while you are eating. And you absolutely *must* practice a down-stay sometime this week while you have company.

Sit-stay for ear cleaning and teeth exam

This is a continuation of our exercises to teach your dog to accept restraint and prevent aggressive responses. When I think of this exercise, I remember a dog in my obedience classes that had a problem with this. Buffy was a difficult-to-handle Cocker Spaniel that was being trained by a thirteen-year-old girl. Buffy's ears were not kept clean, in spite of a Cocker's predisposition to ear problems, because he struggled so much when he was restrained. Partway through the class, he developed a severe ear infection. A trip to the veterinarian resulted in a major battle in order to examine Buffy. Putting in the necessary daily eardrops was next to impossible, which prolonged the infection. After her ears finally cleared up, Buffy returned to class. When her owner reached down to pet her head, Buffy bit her, badly frightening her. A reluctance to be restrained had progressed to aggression. All this could have been prevented with training.

To clean your dog's ears, use a cotton ball or a piece of gauze moistened with mineral oil or isopropyl alcohol and wrapped around your finger. Put your dog on a sit-stay and clean as far as your finger will reach. Because of a dog's L-shaped ear canal, you will not damage the eardrum. I keep a container of medicated acne pads on hand for convenient ear cleaning. Check your dog's ears and clean them regularly to prevent infections. Reward him with a treat for his cooperation.

If you encounter problems with this, start by just handling your dog's ear and putting your finger in his ear. Be stubborn in insisting he stay sitting. Reward when you are successful. Then try just touching his head with the moistened cotton ball or gauze. Some dogs will be frightened by the smell. Work at just touching your dog's head until he is comfortable with it. Then move on to cleaning his ear. Remember Buffy, and don't give up.

Your dog should also allow his teeth to be examined. As dogs are living to an older age with better veterinary care, they have more dental problems. To examine your dog's teeth, start by putting him on a sit-stay. Then close his mouth and gently lift his upper lip up and back. Check the health of his gums as well as his teeth. He should not break his sit-stay.

Handling paws on down-stay

Next week you will be clipping your dog's toenails as part of his training to accept restraint. To prepare for that, here is a warm-up exercise. Down your dog and roll him over onto his side. Then handle each of his paws. Squeeze them as firmly as you will when you cut his toenails. Release him with an "Okay" and reward him.

If you have already tried unsuccessfully to cut your dog's toenails, you may have to overcome toenail clipper phobia. Start by placing the toenail clippers by your dog's bowl when you feed him. Then put your dog on a sit-stay and reward him for staying while you hold the clippers in your hand. When he is comfortable with this, progress to putting him on a down-stay and just touching his toes with the clippers. Be generous with your rewards.

Come from sit-stay

Until now, we have avoided calling your dog from a sit-stay so that he isn't confused about staying. Now we will, in order to practice coming. If your dog doesn't sit and stay well, don't try this.

If your dog doesn't come from a sit-stay, there is little hope of him coming when he is running in the opposite direction. Start with short distances. Put your dog on a sit-stay and go only about six to ten feet away. If he comes before you call him, put him back. If he does this a few times, go back to practicing your sit-stay. Call him ("Max, come") and give him a sit command and hand signal when he gets close. Have a piece of food in your hand ready to reward him. Don't forget to occasionally reach down and take hold of his collar before rewarding him. Extend the distance as your sit-stay permits.

Week 5

Stand-stay for petting and grooming
Down-stay away from home
Heeling with leash tied out of your hands
Toenail clipping

Stand-stay for petting and grooming

Once your dog is comfortable with being placed in a standing position, it is time to introduce the stay. Stand your dog. If you are still using food to get your dog standing, give him the food before you give him the stay command. At first it is probably going to be necessary to steady your dog by keeping your right hand on his collar under his chin, and your left hand under his belly. If he is wiggling all around, give him a shake and repeat the stay command. Make him stay only for a count of five. To help steady him, talk to him in a calm tone of voice. If it helps, gently scratch his belly. Release him and praise.

By now your dog should be starting to understand that "Stay" means freeze in whatever position you are in. However, he may still associate "Stay" with sitting, and may keep trying to sit while you are trying to stand him. Be patient; it is natural for him to be confused at first. If he moves, be careful not to pull on the collar in a way that he would interpret as your asking him to sit. Just reposition him in a stand and try again.

Once he can stand and stay, introduce petting and grooming. When you first ask someone to pet him, kneel beside your dog and have your hands on his collar and stomach to steady him. Have your helper just touch his head. Build up to having him stand for a thorough body examination, running your hands down his back and legs, without your having to hold him. Brush him when he is in a stand-stay and insist he stay. And don't forget to use your stand-stay when at the veterinarian. He or she will be very appreciative!

Down-stay away from home

It is easy to take your dog places with you if he can be put on a down-stay anywhere. You have practiced a down-stay at home with distractions, so this week try it somewhere away from home. A park or a friend's house would be perfect. Do you take your kids to baseball or soccer practice? Take your dog along and make him do a down-stay. Again, be stubborn. He probably won't cooperate at first, so just keep putting him down until he relaxes and stays. It is not unreasonable to ask him to do a down-stay for half an hour, or even longer. One of my introductions to dog training was when I was in college and took my Irish Setter to classes with me, in spite of signs on the doors prohibiting dogs in the buildings. We got away with it because Shauna did an excellent down-stay that lasted the fifty minutes of class. Dogs love to go places, and down-stay training will make that possible.

Heeling with leash tied out of your hands

A good way to test how well you are doing with your heeling training is to heel your dog with the leash tied to you so that you do not have to hold it in your hands. Either tie the leash around your waist or to a belt loop. Adjust the length so there is a little slack but not so much that your dog might trip over it. Then try some heeling. What often happens is that your dog heels better this way. If your dog pulls you, you know he needs more training. If so, it is usually an indication that you are keeping constant tension on the leash by pulling back just a little all the time. If you do this, your dog will be forced to pull against it. This time you have to break *your* bad habit instead of your dog's.

Toenail clipping

Toenail clipping is an essential part of keeping a dog well groomed. It is a procedure that is often ignored by many dog owners. If your dog's toenails click when he walks across a hard surface, they are too long. He should not be walking on his toenails; that is bad for your dog's feet. Because a dog's toenails should be cut every two to four weeks, it is impractical to let this go until a groomer or veterinarian can do it.

Toenail clipping is also an excellent test of your dog's ability to accept restraint. It teaches a dog to tolerate something unpleasant but necessary, a part of many medical treatments. Such training enabled my husband, who is a physician, to stitch up one of our dogs in an emergency situation without anesthesia. A dog who was visiting attacked my Borzoi over a food bowl, lacerating her face, with some of the cuts very close to her eyes. Unfortunately, this happened during a terrible blizzard. It was impossible to get to a veterinarian. Carla cooperated by lying on her side very still while Brad stitched up her face.

Start by downing your dog and laying him on his side. In grasping his paw, be careful not to pull his leg into an unnatural position or get such a death grip on his paw that you are hurting him. If he struggles, do not get someone else to help you hold him. The idea is not to physically hold him in place, but to have training hold him in place. If he struggles too much, go back to last week's lesson and practice some more. Until he gets comfortable with this, you may be able to cut only one toenail at a time. Don't let him get up until you give him the "Okay" command. Then give him a reward.

If your dog has light-colored nails, lucky you. It is easy to see where the quick ends and where to cut. If your dog has dark nails, you will have to guess. The quick generally ends where the nail starts to curve down. Don't panic if you cut a little too much and your dog starts to bleed. If you don't overreact, he won't. Apply some pressure on the nail with a paper towel until the bleeding stops. It is helpful to have on hand a special styptic powder made to stop bleeding toenails.

THE TEST

This test is designed to evaluate the progress you have made with your dog's training. The goal of passing this test will help provide you with motivation to train. If you can't pass all the tests, keep practicing until you can.

To get a more objective evaluation, give a copy of the test to a friend or relative so that they can score you. You may not have food in your hands during any of the tests, but you may have it in your pockets to use as a reward. Remember to use your watch command if you are having trouble getting your dog's attention. If you pass, celebrate—food treats for both you and your dog!

1. **Sitting on command.** You may not touch your dog in any way or have food in your hand. You may give a hand signal.

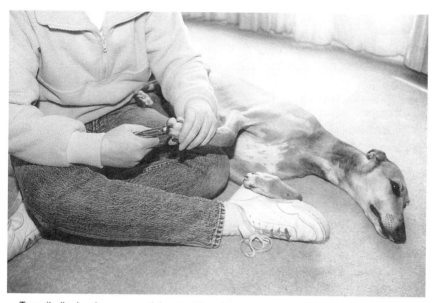

Toenail clipping is an essential part of keeping your dog well-groomed. (Greyhound)

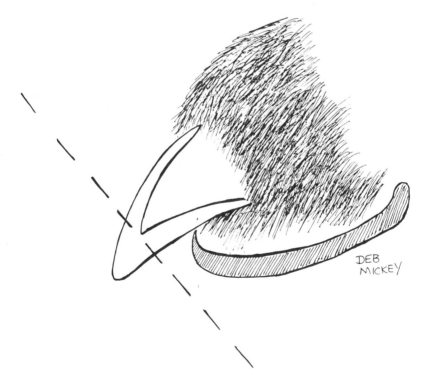

DEB MICKEY

The dotted line indicates the proper place to cut the toenail.

The Test

	Excellent	Fair	Needs Improvement
1. *Sitting on command*	Sits with one command and a small hand signal	Command needs to be repeated or big hand signal needed to get dog's attention	Will not sit without being touched or having collar pulled
2. *Sit-stay off leash, for thirty seconds*	Stays with one command and waits for okay	Needs many commands to remain in place; gets up before okay	Does not stay; gets up or lies down
3. *Sit-stay for petting, off leash*	Stays with one command and waits for okay	Needs many commands to stay; gets up before okay	Does not stay; jumps up
4. *Lying down on command*	Lies down on first command and hand signal	Needs more than one command and signal	Will not lie down without being pushed or pulled down
5. *Heeling on a thread*	Heels without many commands or signals	Needs lots of commands, talking, and signals	Thread breaks
6. *Come and sit*	Stays and comes quickly on first command; sits in front on first command	Needs many commands to stay; needs extra commands to come and to sit	Won't stay; doesn't come; will not sit within arm's reach without being touched
7. *Down-stay for 5 minutes*	Stays down without many extra commands	Needs lots of reminds to stay; gets up but lies back down with minimum of effort	Gets up more than once

2. **Sit-stay, off leash, for thirty seconds.** The distance is optional, but should be at least six feet.

3. **Sit-stay for petting, off leash.** The petting has to be done by someone other than you, of course. Your dog will be sitting in heel position.

4. **Lying down on command.** You may give a hand signal and verbal command, but no food may be in your hand. Whether or not your dog stays down is not to be judged.

5. **Heeling on a thread.** Does your dog really walk on leash without pulling? To find out, attach the leash to the dog's collar by tying them together with a piece of ordinary sewing thread. Heel for about fifty feet.

6. **Come and sit.** Leave your dog on a sit-stay. Do this off leash if you

Never forget to reward your dog for responding to your commands.   (Belgian Tervuren)

have a fenced area, or on a long piece of rope if you do not. Go twenty to thirty feet away and call your dog. You must get him to sit within arm's reach without touching him. Hand signals and commands to sit are okay.

7. **Down-stay for five minutes.** This should be done off leash, if you are indoors, or in a safe place. You should be a few feet away.

TRAINING NEVER ENDS

The more you train your dog, the better your relationship will be. The five weeks of training described in this chapter provide only a foundation that should be built upon with further training. The next chapter will tell you how to enlarge upon the come exercises taught in this chapter to teach your dog to come when called. Five weeks is enough time for your dog to begin to understand what the commands mean, but it is not enough time to achieve any degree of reliability. That only comes with much more practice in different situations with varied distractions.

In order for your dog to retain what he has learned, you must continue training him throughout his lifetime. This reasoning is based on the principle that any learned behavior that is not reinforced will fade or deteriorate. What this means is that if you stop making your dog obey your commands and stop rewarding him for doing so, he will gradually stop obeying them. For instance, if you keep calling your dog to you and never reward him, he will stop coming; if you allow your dog to break a stay without correcting him, he will stop staying.

Training your dog for the rest of his life is not as much work as it may sound because you can and should include your training in your everyday life. This means giving your dog an occasional food reward for the rest of his life. It is not necessary or desirable to ever completely eliminate food rewards for your dog. If you don't keep giving occasional rewards you will find yourself needing to punish him more to get him to listen to your commands. It would be better to prevent this from happening. These rewards do not have to be given every time. In fact, psychologists feel that rewards given irregularly make a behavior stronger.

There are many more commands your dog can learn that would make your relationship with him more enjoyable. Teaching your dog to retrieve on command and deliver to hand is a good example. While such training is not necessary to live with your dog, it sure makes playing with him a lot more fun. Such additional training is beyond the scope of this book, but you can pursue it by reading more books or attending obedience classes. Finding a good class is discussed in Chapter 10.

6

Coming When Called
and the Off-Leash Dog

COMING WHEN CALLED is every dog owner's dream, and most dog owners' nemesis. Yet it is so important to the quality of a dog's life, to a dog's safety, and to a happy relationship between dog and owner. Breathes there a dog owner who has not experienced the horror of chasing a runaway dog? You are filled with anger that it is happening, frustration at your inability to capture an animal that runs faster than you can, and fear that your dog will run out into the street and be hit by a car. And yet some of the biggest pleasures of dog ownership are based on a dog that comes when called off leash—playing Frisbee, going for a quiet walk in the woods, or throwing sticks into a pond for your dog to retrieve. What a contrast of scenes, and it is all dependent on whether or not your dog comes when called.

REALISTIC EXPECTATIONS

Training your dog to come when called will be easier if you start with realistic expectations. When you think about it, what we want is not only that our dogs come when called, but also that they not run away in the first place. What fun would it be to have a dog that always comes when he is called, but as soon as you let him go, he takes off, and you have to call him again? Everyone wants a dog that sticks around or stays in the yard without having to be constantly called. As it turns out, the easiest dog to train to come is the dog that never wants

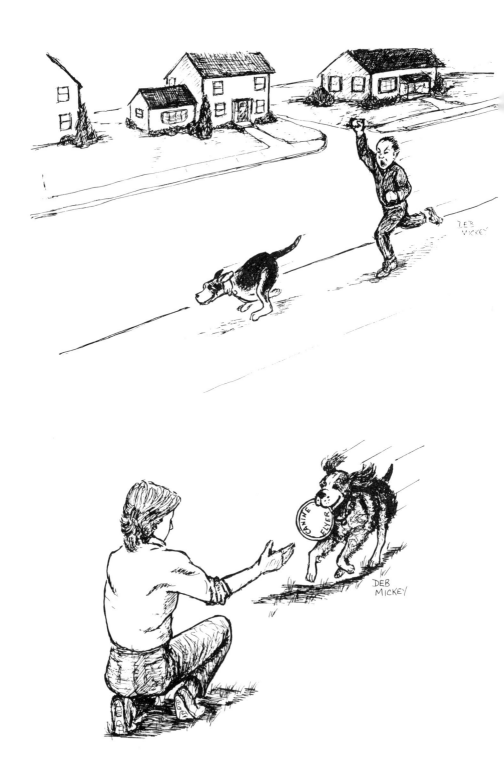

Whether your dog comes to you when called greatly affects your relationship with him.

to leave in the first place, and the hardest one to train is the one that is obsessed with getting away.

Some dogs are easier to train than others. Some dogs will never be safe off leash, and others you couldn't lose if you tried. Knowing what factors affect this will help you to understand your dog and to have realistic expectations regarding his training. Such expectations will help prevent you from feeling angry and frustrated. These emotions interfere with good training by affecting your judgment and your relationship with your dog.

A major factor that determines the ease of training your dog to come when called is the age training is started. The earlier you start, the more you can prevent bad habits from forming. As we have already discussed, puppies have a natural instinct to stay close to their owners and come when called. Starting training early takes advantage of this. With any early start, you can avoid becoming dependent on the leash to get your dog's attention.

Owners who do not start training early get into a vicious cycle. They do not let their dog off leash because he doesn't come when called, so the dog becomes frustrated from lack of exercise and freedom. The frustration builds, so the next time he gets free he will run farther and longer, and the owner is more convinced than ever to never let his dog off leash.

A second factor in training your dog to come when called is your dog's personality, which is partially related to his breed, or mixture of breeds. Of course, not all dogs within a breed are the same, but looking at what the breed was historically bred to do will give you a clue to the ease with which your dog can be trained to come. As a *general rule,* dogs bred to work independently of man and to have a high energy level are harder to train to come when called. Northern breeds, like the Siberian Husky, are difficult because they were bred to run long distances and have independent personalities. Chow Chows are independent and assertive, but fortunately have a lower energy level than Siberians. Sight hounds, which are dogs bred to instinctively chase things that move, love to run and are easily distracted by any moving thing they see. Sight hounds include breeds such as Greyhounds, Afghans, Salukis, Borzois, and Whippets. Doberman Pinschers seem a lot like sight hounds—easily distracted and full of energy. Terriers can be difficult because they are independent and energetic.

Some of the hunting breeds, such as Setters and Pointers, are also hard to train to come because of their innate desire to hunt and their high energy levels. The breeds bred to herd, such as German Shepherds, Border Collies, or Shetland Sheepdogs, are usually the easiest to train because they have little desire to leave in the first place. In between are the rest of the breeds.

The individual personality of your dog will also affect its willingness to come when called. An independent dog is much harder to train than a dependent one, and a bold dog will be more difficult than a shy dog. Females are generally easier to train to come than are males that have not been castrated. Such males are distracted by their hormonally influenced drives. Some dogs have a stronger chase instinct than others and are more likely to run off after a squirrel. A dog doesn't have to be of a hunting breed to like to hunt.

Nancy and Raven. (German Shepherd)

A third factor is the environment in which your dog lives. It is difficult to train a dog to come if he lives in a neighborhood where the houses are close together and the yards are not fenced. The distractions of people, children, cats, and other dogs are too great for most dogs to resist.

I have two friends who have dogs that always come when called, and these dogs are good examples of how these factors work. One is a German Shepherd, and the other is a Golden Retriever. The German Shepherd, Raven, is the kind of dog you couldn't lose if you tried. Her owner and I often go for walks in the woods with our dogs. Her dog comes better than mine do, even though Raven's training consists of just one basic obedience class many years ago and mine have AKC obedience titles and years of training. Her dog is very dependent and just doesn't want to leave her. It is unusual for Raven to get more than twenty-five feet from her owner, and she used to go only a few feet until my dogs encouraged her to go farther. If we come across a squirrel on our walks, my dogs are off and running, but Raven never chases it at all. She has no urge to chase animals. Raven is also a little shy and not attracted to other people, so she doesn't run off to greet neighbors or hikers we meet on the trail. Raven gets long, off-leash walks almost every day, so she gets plenty of exercise, and has since she was a puppy. At home, Raven has a fenced backyard, so there is no problem there.

The Golden Retriever is named Zandy. Zandy lives on property consisting of several acres at the end of a lane quite a distance from the main road. Zandy's owners began taking lessons from me when Zandy was ten weeks old. She has another dog, a cat, two horses, and two children to keep her company and to play with. Her owner does not work and is home all day. Zandy stays in or out as she pleases, and can be trusted to remain around the house without direct supervision. She is an easygoing dog of medium energy level. She is not an adventurous dog and prefers being a follower.

These dogs have several things in common. They are both females of breeds that are generally easy to train to come when called. Both get a lot of off-leash exercise that started when they were young puppies. Neither has strong urges to hunt. They both have dependent personalities and are not bold. Neither are high-energy dogs. In both cases, the fact that they come when called is dependent on factors other than training alone. It is also interesting to note that both are natural retrievers. Natural retrieving instincts seem to be associated with trainability and a willingness on the dog's part to follow his owner's directions.

Before you get too discouraged because your dog isn't the right breed, doesn't have the right personality, and doesn't live in the best situation, let me assure you that you can improve your dog's off-leash responsiveness through good training. But you must have realistic expectations. I have been able to exercise all my dogs off leash, even though they include an Irish Setter, a Borzoi, and a Greyhound—breeds not known for their off-leash obedience. In fact, I have never had a fenced yard, so coming when called is daily work for me and my dogs. In spite of all of their training, if they are chasing a squirrel, I cannot call them and make them stop. However, I can turn my Greyhound loose in an open field and admire her speed and grace as she runs. My husband and I can play

Frisbee with them and take them swimming. Teaching a dog to come when called is hard work, but the rewards are great.

THE FOUNDATION

If you turned to this chapter first before reading the rest of the book because coming when called is a major problem with your dog, you are going to have to go back and read at least the previous chapter. You will do better if you read everything except the housebreaking chapter. The training discussed in this chapter is based on what you have taught your dog from the material presented in the previous chapter. You shouldn't expect your dog to come when he is fifty feet away from you if he doesn't understand what the command means in the first place or if he doesn't respond reliably to it when he is five feet away and on a leash. Make sure your dog will pay attention to you and respond promptly to all the basic commands on leash in the places where you would like him to come when called. The bonding created by the basic training will greatly improve your dog's responsiveness to you in general, which in turn makes it easier to train him to come when called.

Don't make the mistake of skipping the basic training in Chapter 5 because you think that your dog already knows what "come" means. If you haven't made a specific effort to teach him what "come" means, he doesn't. This is a common error because dogs do respond when you call them some of the time, even though they don't know what the word "come" means. In young puppies it is a natural response for them to come toward you when they hear your voice. A dog may know his name and come sometimes when he hears it, but that is not the same as knowing that "come" means to move close enough to you so you could touch him.

UNINTENTIONAL PUNISHMENT: TRAINING YOUR DOG NOT TO COME

Many people unintentionally train their dogs *not* to come. There are many ways to do this, and you want to identify and avoid all of them.

It should be obvious to anyone that calling a dog to you and then punishing him will discourage the dog from coming in the future. If someone called you to them, then slapped you when you got there, would you want to come the next time they called you? While the answer seems obvious, it is hard to control the urge to do just that when you come upon some "evidence of crime" in your house, such as a pillow torn to shreds or a warm puddle. Resist the urge or you will be training your dog not to come. This is the kind of situation we discussed in the first chapter, where anger can overcome reason and add up to bad training.

The situation in which anger is most likely to cause trouble is when your

A dog won't want to come to an angry owner.

dog runs away. For some reason, probably because you are being more careless, this always seems to happen when you are in a hurry. Instead of being on time for your appointment, you find yourself chasing your dog through the neighborhood for half an hour. You keep calling your dog, and he finally comes to you. That's when anger overcomes reason, and you start to punish him, by hitting him, shaking him by his collar, or by yelling at him. What have you really done? You've punished him for coming. This makes it less likely, not more likely, that your dog will come in the future. Nonetheless, some people persist in punishing their dogs in this situation, usually increasing the punishment with each occurrence, even though it is not working. Taken to extremes, this creates a dog that runs away and then *will not* come home out of fear of punishment.

What should you do if you find yourself in this situation? Chalk it up to experience, promise yourself to never let it happen again, grit your teeth, and praise your dog for coming. Okay, you don't have to be enthusiastic. But you have to make sure your dog knows it is safe to come to you should it happen again.

Most situations of unintentional punishment are more subtle. Punishing your dog for coming can be something as simple as just always calling your dog when you want him to come inside. While this may not seem like punishment, if your dog associates being called with his playtime being ended, he is unlikely to want to come. Or perhaps you call him to lock him in his crate before you go to work. Avoid calling your dog for anything he finds unpleasant, such as cutting his toenails or giving him a bath.

Of course, you have to somehow get your dog to come inside, or into his crate, or into the bathtub. There are two solutions to this dilemma. The first is to call him to you, preferably some distance from the back door, the crate, or the bathroom (the final destination), reward him, spend a few minutes petting him, and then lead him by the collar to where you want him.

The second method is to teach your dog a separate command that means to go inside. That way, your command to come is kept separate from any bad associations and is ready when you need it for emergencies. That's what I do. The command I use is "Inside!" For the crate, I use "get in your crate." These commands I can back up with force if my dogs don't obey, and this will not destroy their pleasant associations with the word "come." I use "Inside" for coming into the house and for getting into the car. My dogs seem more willing to obey the inside command than the come command in those situations. It almost seems as if they were confused when I called them to come when they knew that what I really wanted was for them to go inside. Of course, when they come into the house or get in their crates, they often receive a reward.

A variation of training a dog not to come is teaching him to play keep away. We discussed this in the previous chapter, Chapter 5, when you learned how to teach your dog to come, sit, and let you touch his collar. However, it bears repeating again: Don't lunge and grab your dog, and don't chase him when you call him.

THE LONG LINE: A LIFE SAVER

The long line is an important tool in teaching your dog to come when called. It gives your dog a sense of freedom while you maintain control and keep him safe.

The long line is simply a thirty- to forty-foot leash. It is also called a check cord. It can be made of many different materials and can either be purchased ready-made or made by yourself. Cotton or nylon webbing, any kind of rope, or nylon cord can be used along with a well-fitting buckle collar that will not slip over your dog's head if your dog pulls on it. A dog that charges to the end of a forty-foot rope and is wearing a choke collar may damage his neck when he hits the end of it.

I like polypropylene rope of about ⅜-inch width because it is strong enough for a medium- to large-size dog but not overly heavy and it doesn't tangle easily. It also doesn't soak up moisture like cotton webbing does. You can just buy thirty to forty feet of rope in a hardware store and a medium-size bolt snap to tie onto the end of it. Make sure the bolt snap is no larger than necessary to hold your dog. Getting an enormous, heavy bolt snap that would hold an elephant and acts as an anchor for your dog to drag around defeats the purpose of the long line. You want the dog to have a sense of freedom, and this would be negated by dragging around a heavy rope with a big bolt snap. If you have a small dog, you will have to use a lightweight cord and a very small bolt snap. For small dogs I use parachute cord that I purchase at an army surplus store. Unfortunately, it tangles easily.

WHEN TO USE THE LONG LINE

The long line is used after you have taught your dog the meaning of the word "come," off leash, in a confined area, and you are ready to move to a place where your dog may not come. Start in a place with a minimum of distractions.

Just because your dog zooms to you whenever you call him in the house, do not assume that he knows what you mean when you call him outside. When the situation changes by moving from a familiar situation, such as inside the house or in a fenced backyard, to a new place, your dog may not understand what you want. He only associates the command with a particular place and it may take him a while to learn what the "come" command means in a new place and situation. Be patient, and don't be frustrated by this temporary relapse.

The long line is a good tool to use when a puppy outgrows the stage where he naturally sticks close to his owner. You will know when it is time. It usually happens between the ages of twelve and sixteen weeks. Your puppy looks up when you call, and turns and heads in the opposite direction. If you have done a lot of early puppy training, this stage may be delayed until a later age. When this happens, do not yell and scream and chase after your puppy. Calmly walk toward him and keep walking after him until you can call him to you and take hold of his collar. If he is heading in a dangerous direction, loudly call his name and run in the opposite direction, encouraging him to chase you. Then do not let him off the long line for the next two to four weeks.

Not every dog needs to be trained on a long line. With the right dog in the right environment and the proper early puppy training, you may be able to skip it.

HOW TO USE THE LONG LINE

The most important rule in using the long line is to avoid keeping constant tension on it. Your dog should not pull you around on it, and neither should you pull your dog. Keeping tension on the line destroys the feeling of freedom you are trying to give your dog. It is best if you do not hold on to the line at all, but let your dog drag it around. If, however, you think your dog will bolt and run even with the long line on, by all means hang on to the end of it. If you have to do this, wear gloves to prevent rope burns.

Don't forget to have a pocketful of treats when you take your dog out on the long line. Wait until his back is turned to you, or he is distracted by sniffing at something. Call his name to get his attention, then give him the command "Come!" Remember to give him consistent commands, using the exact same words and *same tone of voice* as you used when teaching him to come and sit for food. Make your commands sound inviting, not like a drill sergeant's order.

If your dog turns toward you when he hears his name and starts toward you, praise him like crazy all the way in and drop down to your knees to receive him with open arms. Be super enthusiastic with your praise, and give him a treat. Sometimes it is good to dispense with the formality of the sit and just let him plow into you.

If your dog does not turn toward you when he hears his name and the come command, give him a sharp tug on the line. Do not use the line to drag him in like a fish on a line. Keep giving him sharp tugs on the line and encouraging him with your voice until he starts coming on his own. When he gets there, even though he needed help, praise him and give him a treat. Most likely at this stage of the game he doesn't understand what you want, so you must help him understand by rewarding him when he gets to you.

After your dog receives his praise and treat, it is very important that you then release him with an "okay" command and allow him to move around freely again. You want your dog to think that "come" means "time to take a break and get a treat," not "this is the end of playtime." Remember, don't unintentionally punish your dog for coming by always using the command to end your dog's playtime.

Once your dog is responding well on the long line, so well that you don't feel you need to hold on to the line, it is time to make the training more challenging by adding distractions. Take him out on the long line while the neighborhood gang of six-year-olds is running around screaming, and call him

The long line is a useful tool for teaching your dog to come.   (Airedale)

away if he tries to join in. Leave a piece of bread lying in the yard. Casually approach the area where the bread is until your dog is sniffing or eating it. Then call him. Again, give him a good tug on the line if he doesn't start toward you. It is okay if he brings the piece of bread with him when he comes, just as long as he comes.

If you walk your dog in a park and let him play with other dogs, let him play with the long line on, then occasionally call him to you for a treat. Be careful not to jerk the line if any of the other dogs are tangled up in it.

As mentioned earlier, teaching a dog to come when called also involves teaching him how far he can go from you by calling him when he gets too far away. Walk him around the perimeter of your yard and correct him if he steps over the line. Remember to keep the line slack; don't tighten up on the line as he approaches the boundary of your yard and prevent him from leaving. Let him step over the line, then say ''No, come!'' If he does, praise him profusely. If he doesn't, give him a jerk on the line. Keep repeating this until the lesson is learned.

For some dogs, this may be as far as they progress. They may always have to be on a long line for their own safety. Some may be safe to take off leash in some places and not in others. For instance, many dogs may be fine off leash in a big, open field while you are keeping them busy with a game of Frisbee but they cannot be trusted in their own unfenced backyards with the distractions of other dogs and people and the danger of a street close by. A good compromise, if you don't have a fenced yard, may be to take your dog to another place several times a week for off-leash exercise.

THE OFF-LEASH DOG

Hopefully, your long line work will progress until you are ready to try some off-leash work. You should first be comfortable with giving your dog a lot of freedom on the long line. You may want to gradually reduce your and your dog's dependence on the long line by reducing its weight and its length, until your dog is dragging a three-foot piece of lightweight cord.

Your chances of being successful when you take your dog off leash can be increased by setting up the situation to your advantage. Choose the best place and the best time. First of all, dogs always come better when called in unfamiliar places. Some suggestions for testing your dog's training are a friend's fenced backyard or a tennis court that is entirely fenced. If you are starting in an unfenced area, make sure you are far from a road. Watch out for wildlife that your dog might chase. I prefer to use a trail in a wooded area rather than a big, open field. The disadvantage of an open field is that a dog can see farther than in the woods and may chase something he sees quite a distance away. Dogs can detect movement farther away than people can. Also, your dog can get quite a distance from you yet still have the security of being able to see you. The turns in a wooded trail help prevent a dog from getting too far ahead because he won't be able to see you.

134

The best time to try your dog off leash is in warmer weather. The heat will decrease his endurance.

It helps if your dog has already been thoroughly exercised *before* you take the leash off. An hour's worth of jogging would be best, but if that's not possible, try a long walk in the area where you intend to let him off leash.

Increase your dog's motivation by bringing special food treats with you and making sure he is hungry. Don't use your everyday training treats. How would your dog feel about slices of pepperoni? I'll never forget what one student brought for her dog's first time off leash. The dog was a Borzoi, which had been kept on a chain in the backyard most of his life. He and his owner had successfully completed a basic obedience class. When she showed up at the place at which we had decided to meet, she got out of the car with an *entire roasted chicken* wrapped in aluminum foil!

It helps to have dogs along that are very good about coming when called and don't like getting far from their owners. Having other dogs to play with will motivate your dog to stay with the group.

The first time Shannon, an adult Golden Retriever–Irish Setter mix, was taken off leash is a good example of setting up the situation for success. Shannon lives with her owner at a horse stable. Unfortunately, even though Shannon lived on several acres, whenever she got loose outside she ran across the road. When her owner finally caught her after a long chase, he punished her. This resulted in Shannon staying away longer and longer, and becoming harder and harder to catch. It also resulted in Shannon's gaining a tremendous amount of weight from lack of exercise.

After some basic training, we were ready to try Shannon off leash. We started out by jogging her on leash about a mile on a warm day. Because Shannon had received little exercise lately, she was in poor shape and got tired easily. Then we walked Shannon to the far end of the stable property along with two dogs who were friendly with other dogs and pretty good about coming when called. Shannon's owner filled his pockets with slices of hot dogs and made sure Shannon knew they were there. Then we turned Shannon loose and started walking. It is much easier to keep a dog with you if you are walking somewhere, than if you are just standing still. If you are walking, your dog is occupied with keeping up with you and cannot get too distracted, but if you stand still, many dogs will gradually drift away and become involved in pursuing their own interests.

Shannon did fine. Her owner called her back every couple of minutes, gave her a slice of hot dog, and released her to continue playing. The hardest part was keeping her owner from panicking every time Shannon got more than a few feet away. When we walked back and got close to the road, we called Shannon in and put her on leash. Shannon cannot be turned loose at the stable without supervision, as their previous dog could, but at least she can get some exercise off leash.

Once you have been successful in letting your dog off leash, you have broken the cycle of your dog running away because of lack of exercise and freedom. Prevent the cycle from starting again by keeping him exercised. It is helpful to occasionally let your dog run until he is tired, instead of stopping when *you* want to quit. You can gradually give him more freedom in more challenging situations.

KEEPING UP YOUR COME TRAINING

Training your dog to come never really ends. As with anything you teach your dog, any behaviors that are not reinforced, either by reward or punishment, will gradually disappear, and that includes coming when called. However, unlike losing your dog's training to not pull on the leash, losing your come training may cost your dog his life.

The first rule is not to wait until your dog stops coming when called to do something about it. Maintain your come training. Always reward your dog for coming when you call him. Praise him enthusiastically every single time. Never take his coming for granted. Every once in a while, give him a food reward. Try not to call him more than four times without giving him a reward.

You need to know what to do if your dog doesn't come when you call him when he is off leash *after* he has been trained. First of all, don't keep calling him, repeating the command. This will just teach him to ignore you. You will be untraining your dog by calling him repeatedly and allowing him to ignore your commands. And don't chase after him, unless it is an emergency. Don't change your tone of voice. If you sound angry or scared, he will be less likely to come to you. He may not even recognize the command if your tone of voice is different.

There are times you can punish your dog if he does not come and improve his response. This must be done the right way and at the right time to be effective. You must not do this until you are absolutely sure that your dog understands what "come" means. He must have been responding to the command most of the time in a majority of situations before you attempt to punish him when he does not come.

If your dog is sniffing around and ignoring you, just walk up to him quietly. I find that if I am ready to explode with anger, I can sometimes cover it up by humming quietly as I approach. Then, once I get my hands on my dog, I repeat the "come" command so my dog knows why he is being disciplined and give him a good shake or jerk on the collar.

Sometimes things aren't that easy. I remember the first time my Greyhound puppy ignored my "Inside" command. It was a lovely day, and she just didn't want to stop playing. I was in an irritated mood. She took one look at me, knew what mood I was in, and became determined not to be caught with all the defiance a five-month-old puppy could muster. Now how much chance do you think I had of catching a dog bred to sprint at forty miles an hour? I took a deep breath, tried to tell myself it was a wonderful training opportunity even though it was going to make me late and disrupt my entire day, accepted the fact that I couldn't change it anyway, and started humming as I walked after her. We went

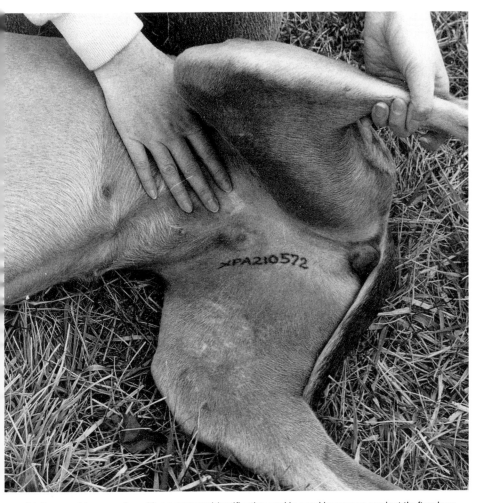

A tattoo provides your dog with permanent identification and is good insurance against theft or loss.

in circles around the house for forty-five minutes. I didn't want to call her to me at this point because if she came to me I would have to praise her. She finally stopped, and I could walk up to her and take hold of her collar. At that point I repeated the "Inside" command, gave her a very hard shake, and abruptly marched her into the house. I was very dramatic in order to impress her. I never again had trouble getting her to come inside.

Watch for little signs that the training is fading. The first sign is usually that he stops coming on the first command, but waits until you have called him several times. Then you find yourself getting louder. If you find your dog frequently ignoring your command to come, and a few corrections don't work, go back to the long line for a refresher course. Don't be lazy; go after your dog and get him when he doesn't come.

Fenced yards can be an enemy of training a dog to come because you don't often need to call your dog if he is always in a fenced yard or in the house. Your dog won't get much practice. Be careful to keep up the training.

Remember that anytime you take your dog off leash you are taking a chance. Make sure your dog is well identified in case he is separated from you. The best form of identification is tattooing. A tattoo is a permanent identification number placed on the inside of a dog's thigh. This number can be tattooed on your dog without anesthesia. While dogs find it uncomfortable, most dogs don't act as if it is more distressing than having their toenails trimmed. They are mostly frightened of being restrained and having the hair clipped from their thigh. Done properly by someone experienced, tattooing takes only a few minutes. This number should then be registered with a national registry so that it can be traced if your dog is lost. For more information on tattoos, contact your veterinarian, a local Humane Society, or check the classifieds of dog magazines.

In spite of all the training, there is always a possibility of your dog running into the street and being hit by a car. I know my dogs get more minor injuries, such as cuts and sprains, because they are allowed the freedom to play off leash. Balancing concern for your dog's safety with concern for the quality of his life is a difficult decision to make.

7

Exercise: The Magic Problem Solver

THE MEMBERS of the genus *canis,* which includes wolves, coyotes, jackals, and domestic dogs, are predators that hunt by traveling long distances looking for prey and then chasing them. Wolves, a close wild relative of dogs, can travel an average of fifteen miles a day. Dogs, except for those breeds that have been radically changed by man's selective breeding, have the endurance and energy of their wild ancestors. Problems arise when this energy is not given an outlet.

Dogs that do not get enough exercise become frustrated. This frustration often causes undesirable behaviors: chewing, barking, digging, running away, and general unruliness, to name a few. Almost any behavior problem can be improved by providing a dog with more exercise. A tired dog doesn't need to find an outlet for his energy. He is less likely to get into trouble. A tired dog is a well-behaved dog.

All the training in the world is not a substitute for adequate exercise. Even though training can tire a dog, it cannot relax a dog the way exercise can. Training and exercise depend on each other. It is hard to exercise a dog that pulls on the leash and won't come when called. On the other hand, it is hard to train a dog that hasn't had enough exercise.

Providing a dog with adequate exercise is not easy. You come home from a hard day at work, ready to collapse, only to be faced with a dog that has been sleeping all day and is now bursting with energy. However, this is a sacrifice you should be prepared to make if you own a dog. If you can see it as a time for you to relax, too, it won't seem like so much of a chore.

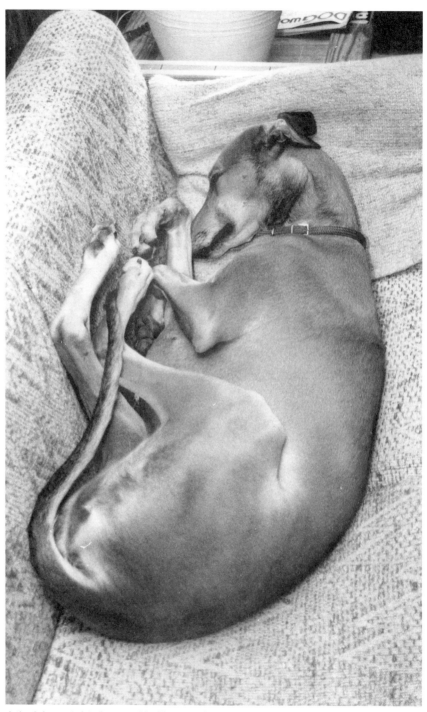

A tired dog gets into less trouble (if you don't count sleeping on the furniture!) (Greyhound)

HOW MUCH?

The amount of exercise a dog needs is different for every dog and depends on various factors. Some of these factors were discussed in Chapter 4. Obviously, a dog with a high energy level needs more exercise. Your dog's breed will have an effect on his need for exercise. Among those breeds developed for tireless activity are sled dogs, hunting dogs, and herding dogs. An older dog needs less exercise than a younger dog. Another factor is whether your dog is an only dog or has another dog to encourage him to play and exercise.

A dog's exercise needs do *not* depend on his size. Small dogs do not necessarily need less exercise than large dogs. Some large dogs, especially some of the giant breeds, are very phlegmatic, while a small terrier can be like a missile on four legs. A Mastiff may only need a leisurely stroll around the block, while a Jack Russell Terrier may be going strong after two miles of brisk walking.

Like humans, dogs derive the most health and mental benefits from exercise if it is extended aerobic exercise, not just a fast sprint. Don't make the mistake of thinking that because your dog is panting, he is tired and should stop exercising. Dogs pant to cool themselves, much like we sweat. It does not mean they are gasping for oxygen.

Access to a fenced yard is not enough to provide most dogs with adequate exercise. They won't exercise on their own, other than perhaps a fast dash around the yard with the initial burst of energy. Left alone in a yard for long periods, they become bored and can develop behavior problems, such as digging or excessive barking. Even more useless for exercise than access to a fenced yard is being tied out on a chain or an overhead trolley.

Exercise must be limited for dogs with physical problems, puppies, and old dogs. Puppies need short, frequent bursts of exercise, and should never be forced to exercise longer than they wish. As dogs get older they need less exercise. Old dogs derive many health benefits from regular exercise, even if they don't need it from a behavioral viewpoint. A brisk walk of a mile may be just the thing for a ten-year-old dog, even if he has arthritis and reduced heart function. Exercise encourages regular bowel movements, keeps up muscle tone, preserves range of motion in the joints, and provides much needed mental stimulation. When deciding about cutting back on an older dog's exercise, keep in mind that dogs age at different rates, with large dogs having shorter life spans and showing signs of age earlier than small dogs.

Whenever you are exercising your dog, you must be careful about the heat. Dogs do not cool as efficiently as humans because they cannot sweat through their skin. As mentioned above, a dog cools itself by panting, which circulates blood through the lungs and nose where it comes into contact with cooler surfaces. When you are hot, your dog is hotter. An overheated dog can die of heatstroke.

So what is a good amount of exercise for your dog? Let his behavior tell you. Is he relaxed or restless? Think about any behavior problems your dog may have. Is the cause lack of training, or is it lack of exercise? Most likely it is a combination of both. However, if inadequate exercise is part of the cause, training alone will not solve your problem. The answer is giving your dog more exercise.

WALKING YOUR DOG: GOOD FOR BOTH OF YOU

The classic way to exercise your dog is walking him on leash. If this is the way you are going to exercise your dog, make sure exercising is what you are doing and not just giving him a chance to relieve himself on the neighbors' lawns. Walk briskly and do not allow him to stop. He should relieve himself at home before you leave.

Train your dog to walk without pulling, then never allow him to pull again when you are walking him. It is not good for your dog to be dragging you down the street, gasping and wheezing for air. And it is not good for your arm! You will have to be stubborn, because it is not natural for an excited dog to walk at a slow enough pace to match yours. Make sure that anyone who walks him insists on him not pulling; consistency is important if walking without pulling is going to become a habit. If you walk your dog in an open area, you may want to try walking him on a retractable leash. It will give him a little more freedom, and he won't pull as much.

Greyhounds used for coursing rabbits in England were walked five to ten miles a day. Now that's a walk! You may not want to do as much, but remember that extended exercise is best for your dog. This means at least twenty minutes of walking for a little dog, and more for a larger dog. Two miles would be good for medium and large dogs.

A wonderful aspect of walking your dog on leash, even if it isn't as efficient as exercising a dog off leash, is that it often gives you an opportunity to meet people. You may even meet someone with whom you can form a dog play group!

DOG PLAY GROUPS

On the first night of my puppy training classes I tell all the owners to take the leashes off their puppies and let them play. At first no one wants to do it. They are afraid there will be fights or a puppy will be hurt. With a lot of persuasion, and often by unsnapping the leashes myself, the puppies are turned loose and start to play. And the owners start to smile. It is fun to watch the puppies run and wrestle and tumble around the room, having the time of their lives. Some of the puppies may be a little shy at first, but they join in eventually.

After a few minutes of play time, we begin class with puppies that are more able to concentrate because they aren't bursting with energy. After class, the puppies are rewarded with another play session. The owners are rewarded with tired puppies that go home and collapse. I also try to have a playtime after the

A dog play group is a good way to provide your dog with exercise.

beginners class for dogs over five months old. Because the dogs are older, not all of them will want to play. There may be two uncastrated males that are likely to fight if given the opportunity. Or there may be a dog that has lacked socialization with other dogs to the extent that he or she cannot interact normally with other dogs. After these dogs leave, the rest of the dogs are allowed to play.

You can also exercise your dog this way and provide him with the opportunity to socialize with members of his own species by forming a dog play group. This is a group of dogs that get together to play on a regular but informal basis. It is especially beneficial for a dog that doesn't live with another dog. You can start by just getting together with one other dog and owner, and add more as interest develops. Whether the group meets every morning or only once a week or month, any opportunity for your dog to play is better than none.

The advantage of a regular play group is that your dog will play better with dogs he knows well. As the dogs become better friends, they will become less inhibited with each other in their interactions. They will get to know what games the other dogs like to play and what behavior they will or will not tolerate. The dogs will develop their own special games, complete with elaborate rules that escape a human's understanding. They will even develop special friendships. A regular play group is especially helpful if your dog tends to be uncomfortable or even aggressive around dogs he doesn't know.

The dogs will get along better if they are off leash. A leash prevents dogs from being able to communicate normally because it restricts their body language. Dogs are more likely to fight if they are on leash. In fact, a dog who behaves aggressively toward other dogs when he is on leash may be fine with other dogs when he is off leash. If a dog has to be on leash, it is best to use a long line.

Dog play groups can meet in a variety of places. It is best if you select a site where the dogs can be off leash. Public places should be avoided except during off hours. A pack of dogs playing together can be very frightening to some people. Sometimes the dog owners in a development can meet in an empty lot at the end of the development. A dog owner without a fenced yard may be grateful for an opportunity to let his dog off leash in someone's fenced yard. Tennis courts may be good when they are not being used. And you don't have to stand still while the dogs are playing. One of the things I enjoy most in life is to go for a hike in the woods with a group of friends and their dogs. It is not unusual for us to have six to eight dogs along, and we once had sixteen!

Dog play groups can be combined with dog training. Besides providing you with an opportunity to train your dog around the distractions of other dogs, you can get advice from the other owners. It is more fun to train as part of a group than by yourself. Don't forget to line all the dogs up on a sit-stay and take a picture of your dog with his buddies.

It is likely that when dogs play together there may be a fight. They are usually not serious, although they may sound horrible. Dogs rarely hurt each other in a fight, if neither dog has a severe psychological problem and if they have enough space to separate. If one occurs, do not scream and get hysterical.

That will only make the fight worse. Wait a few seconds and see if it will resolve itself without your interference. Then try yelling loudly in a firm tone of voice and telling them to stop. If this doesn't work, separate them by grabbing their tails and pulling. You can also grab the skin and fur on the back of a dog's neck to separate them. Do not reach in and try to grab for collars. That is a good way to get your hand in the way of their mouths and get bitten.

When you become more skilled at reading dog body language, you will be able to see the fights developing and warn the dogs to behave before the fight happens. This requires a dog who is very responsive to commands, however. Typically in our play group, the male dogs will start stalking each other. We just warn them with "Boooys . . .," and because the dogs are trained, they separate and find something else to do.

Don't mistake rough play for fighting. There can be a lot of growling and biting between good friends. A student of mine says people have come to her door to warn her that her dogs were killing each other in her backyard when they were only playing. It amazes me to watch my two dogs, Zephyr and Sabre, chew on each other. Zephyr has the typical, tissue-paper thin, fragile skin of a Greyhound that seems to split open incredibly easily. However, Sabre has never broken her skin in even their roughest wrestling matches.

Avoid giving the dogs toys if they might fight over them. However, sometimes an old rag can stimulate a good game of tug-of-war or catch-me-if-you-can. Dogs who won't chase a ball normally may do so when there is another dog to compete with.

Watching dogs play is entertaining and relaxing. It is fascinating to observe their behavior with each other and how they communicate. You can learn a lot about dog body language. And you will probably spend more time exercising your dog if you have company. Everybody benefits from a dog play group!

JOGGING WITH YOUR DOG

I was surprised the other day to talk to someone who thought it was cruel to make a dog jog with you. She ought to be at my house when my husband starts to get dressed to go jogging. The canine jogging addicts I live with go crazy. They spin through the house like whirling dervishes, whining in anticipation, both hoping to be the first to go. Age having its privileges, it is the custom in our house for the oldest dog to go first. So Sabre lunges out the door, biting at the leash in his anxiety to get started.

Good heeling is a must for jogging, and it can be a challenge to teach a dog not to get excited and pull when you are running. Your dog has to understand that he cannot lunge after squirrels that cross your path or fight with dogs that might chase you. A prong collar often provides a good solution. Be careful if you are using a buckle collar that your dog cannot pull back out of it if he is startled. Since you are more visible than your dog, you will want to jog so that you are the one closest to the traffic. This means that if your dog is used to heeling on the left, you will have to jog facing traffic.

The author's husband, Brad, jogging with his Belgian Tervuren, Sabre.

Not all dogs like or should be jogging. Puppies should be at least eight months old before you begin, and older if they are a large, heavy-boned dog. Jogging is obviously not suitable for very small dogs. Dogs with hip dysplasia should jog only if a veterinarian has first been consulted. It may be that jogging moderate distances may build muscles that would help a dysplastic dog. If you have a breed prone to hip dysplasia, which includes most large breeds, avoid jogging if there is any sign of a limp or even a problem keeping up with you. Again, consult a veterinarian to be sure. Never force a dog to jog.

How far you run with your dog is determined by your dog's and your condition. Two miles is probably a good distance, but even one mile of jogging can have a big effect on your dog's behavior. The maximum distance my husband has ever run with our dogs is 6.2 miles, the distance of a ten-kilometer race, which they sometimes do together. A dog must be over one year of age to do this kind of distance, and we advocate reducing the distance as the dog gets over eight years old. Elderly dog jogging addicts can be a problem, as it is hard to explain to them that they are too old to continue jogging. We deal with the problem by taking our senior citizens over ten years old on "pretend jogs." These are slow jogs of one-quarter to one-half mile to pacify the dog before leaving on the real run.

As mentioned before, be careful about the heat when jogging. Increases in temperature decrease your dog's endurance faster than it does yours because his body does not cool as efficiently. He cannot sweat. When temperatures rise over 75 degrees, it is probably a good idea to leave your dog at home—even if that means you have to sneak out the door so that your canine jogging addict doesn't go berserk!

Be careful also as your distances increase that the pads on your dog's feet are up to it, especially if you run on hard surfaces. This is true whether you are jogging or walking your dog. Dogs' pads vary in their toughness; check the pads often. Hot pavement can blister a dog's feet. The road can remain hot even after the air has cooled.

The satisfaction some dogs derive from jogging transcends the exercise they receive. It is as if they have found the domestic equivalent of setting out on the hunt. A faraway look comes into their eyes; they ignore all distractions, intent on just covering ground. Dog and human become comrades in pursuit of their destination.

FINDING A PLACE TO EXERCISE OFF LEASH

Off-leash exercise is the most relaxing kind of exercise for a dog. Free from restraint, a dog can really be a dog. You can enjoy the beauty and expression of their movements. However, finding a place you can safely and legally do this is difficult.

Finding a good place often requires some detective work. Ask other dog owners where they exercise their dogs. A farmer might give you permission to use his fields when the crops aren't growing. If you have a friend who is a realtor, he may be able to tell you where there is vacant land for sale that you can use until it is sold.

Trails where you and your dog can walk together are good for off-leash exercise. Keeping your dog with you when he is off leash is easier if you are going somewhere, not just standing still. Walking also encourages your dog to exercise more. People who like to hike may also be able to give you some tips, as may books on local hiking trails. Look for side trails off the more popular trails where you can avoid bothering other people. Buy a topographic map and peruse it for old logging trails. Check out state gamelands and snowmobile trails. Ask a hunter, especially one who hunts with dogs, for suggestions. Be careful if you are using areas where people hunt; know when the various hunting seasons start and end so you can avoid being out during those times.

While parks are more convenient for exercising than the alternatives mentioned above, they must be used with great care and caution. It is almost always against the law or rules of the park to let your dog off leash. You will be able to do so only if you are very careful to avoid infringing on the rights of other park users. Any time you have your dog off leash, it is of paramount importance that you respect the rights of nondog owners. Previous failure to do so on the part of many dog owners has resulted in greater and greater restrictions on the places our dogs can go. Your dog has to be very responsive to your commands, never wandering far from you and always coming when called. In a park, other people and dogs present a strong distraction that makes control of your dog difficult. Visiting a park during off hours, either early in the morning or at dusk, is a good idea. The city of Berkeley probably has the best idea; it has set up a special dog park.

You must also respect the rights of dog owners who keep their dogs on leash and may not want other dogs near them. As the owner of a dog who is sometimes aggressive with other dogs, I know it is infuriating to have to lift Sabre off his front feet by means of his collar and let him strangle while another dog who is off leash runs around him, ignoring his owner's commands to come and eluding all attempts at capture.

Hopefully, it is not necessary to remind you that you must clean up after your dog. My favorite cleanup method is a plastic bag pulled over my hand like a glove. Once the stool is picked up, you can pull the plastic bag back over your hand and knot it. They are convenient to carry in your pocket. Use a part of the park that is least used, away from eating areas and places where children play. Keep in mind that even if you clean up after your dog, left in the grass is some residue that picnickers shouldn't have to sit in or children play in.

If you are going to exercise your dog off leash, there is always a risk that he will become separated from you and lost, so good identification is a must. The best form of identification is a tattoo, which was described in the previous chapter. Even if your dog is not exercised off leash, a tattoo is still a good idea. It is insurance against your dog being stolen. Dog theft is a multimillion-dollar business in this country. Stolen dogs are sold to dealers, who in turn sell them

Biking a dog. (Golden Retriever)

to laboratories. Since laboratories do not buy tattooed dogs, such dogs aren't stolen; if they are, they are turned loose. Tattooing is not expensive, and is the best insurance that, if you ever lose your dog, he will be returned.

Even if it means driving a half hour to get there, or spending a lot of time training your dog to come when called, you and your dog will both be happier if he can get some off-leash exercise.

OTHER ALTERNATIVES

Riding a bike while your dog runs along beside you on leash is another alternative for providing your dog with exercise. It requires teaching your dog to heel with a bicycle, and must be done in places without much traffic, either vehicular or pedestrian. You should keep your speed at a comfortable pace for your dog, so he can keep up with you at a trot and not have to run. This could be done in a deserted parking lot in the evening. A German endurance test requires a dog to trot beside his owner on a bicycle for twelve miles, and then perform a few obedience exercises at the end of it. This test must be passed before a German Shepherd can be bred in Germany.

In hot weather, swimming is a good form of exercise. It is great exercise for older dogs with arthritis, because the joints do not have to bear weight while they are being used. You will probably have to get into the water yourself to teach your dog to enjoy swimming. While most dogs will swim if they fall into deep water, dogs will rarely step off into water over their heads to swim without encouragement from their owners. With a few lessons, however, they usually learn to love it.

If you cannot exercise your dog yourself, consider hiring a dog walker. You will miss out on the benefits to your relationship that exercising your dog provides, but at least your dog won't be frustrated. Your dog walker could be a neighborhood child who wants to earn some money. You can give your dog walker a prescribed route to follow for these walks, or he could just throw a ball for your dog in your backyard. This is a good alternative for a single person who works during the day and has occasional commitments in the evening that would preclude any time for walking a dog, or for an older person.

Although training does not have the same relaxing effects as other forms of exercise, it can tire out a rambunctious dog. There may be times that your dog needs to be exercised but you cannot go far from home. Just run through the exercises described in Chapter 5. Do them at a brisk pace. If pouring rain makes the prospect of a walk less than thrilling, try training indoors. Heel around the dining room table. Practice your stays. Try leaving the room while your dog is on a down-stay. Take turns with another family member calling him from different rooms of the house. Teach him a trick. How about jumping a small barrier set up in a hallway or a doorway? Make sure you do this on a carpet so he doesn't slip.

Be creative in solving your exercise problems. For instance, if your dog likes to retrieve but you cannot throw a ball any distance, try hitting a tennis ball with a tennis racket. You can practice coming when called and exercise your dog at the same time if you have another person with whom to call your dog back and forth. Don't forget the food rewards! When we lived in Vermont and had to cope with a long winter, we exercised our dogs by taking them cross-country skiing.

I use a combination of ways to exercise my dogs. They get to jog with my husband about twice a week for about two and a half miles apiece. Once a week we like to take them for a long hike in the woods for several hours, preferably with other dogs along for company. This does as much for our mental relaxation as it does for theirs. The other four days of the week our busy schedule limits the time we can exercise them. On these days we drive them to a nearby open field so our Greyhound can sprint to her heart's content, and then we play a fast game of Frisbee or ball.

THE BENEFITS OF EXERCISE

This chapter has emphasized the behavioral reasons to exercise your dog, but there are many health reasons as well. Your dog's weight gives you a big clue about whether or not he is getting enough exercise. Just like people, dogs that get exercise and keep their weight down are healthier and live longer.

Exercising your dog can have special benefits just for you. It will force you to take a break from the frantic rush of modern life. The time that my husband and I spend exercising our dogs together is often our only chance for uninterrupted conversation. Exercising your dog will encourage you to get exercise that you might not get otherwise. Even though you are tired when you get home from work, walking your dog may be just the thing you need to wind down and relax.

There is something special about the bond you form with your dog when you exercise together. You are meeting one of his most basic needs. You are not making demands on him like you are when you are training him. It is quality time. Exercising your dog is an expression of your love for him.

8

Common Behavior Problems

"Max get down. Get down! Oh, no, my new silk dress is ruined."

"Honey, you better come into the living room. You're not going to believe what Toby did to the sofa."

"Hi. Come on in. I'll have to put Fifi in the bedroom so we can talk. She won't stop barking."

"Oh, Mitzi won't let you touch her. She doesn't like men, children, or women in hats."

I F THESE LINES sound familiar, maybe you have some of the behavior problems covered in this chapter: jumping up, destructive chewing, excessive barking, and shyness. Combined with housebreaking, not coming when called, pulling on leash, and biting, which are covered elsewhere in this book, these are the most common reasons people call me for help with their dogs. They are also the reasons many dogs are destroyed daily in animal shelters.

There are rarely quick fixes for behavior problems, because these are usually symptoms of more complicated underlying problems that need to be solved, most involving miscommunication between owner and dog. If you haven't read the previous chapters, you will need to read Chapter 1 to understand why punishment won't work and Chapter 4 to understand the effects of your dog's personality on the problems you are having. The training described in Chapter 5 is an important tool in solving any problem because it builds a foundation of communication. Armed with basic training and understanding, you can attack the problem. However, the discussions of the behavior problems presented here are by necessity simplified. Additionally, there are dog behavior problems that could not be covered. If this chapter does not help you solve your problem, do not hesitate to consult a professional.

JUMPING UP

Jumping up is the behavior problem listed most frequently on the registration sheets for my obedience classes. It is a good behavior problem to have, because it means you have a normal, friendly dog. I'd be concerned about the temperament of a dog, especially a puppy, that *didn't* want to jump up. As I said above, there is no magic cure for this problem, like stepping on his toes or hitting him in the chest with your knee. While these methods sometimes work, they can make your dog afraid of you, and they probably will not stop him from jumping up on other people. Instead, you should teach your dog how you want him to greet people, not violently punish him for greeting you or someone else in his own natural body language.

Your dog's personality will affect the degree of difficulty in training him not to jump up. Dogs that are excitable naturally find it difficult to control themselves in exciting situations like their owner's return or meeting new people. High-energy dogs have the same problem of self-control. Lots of exercise will help these dogs with their jumping-up problem. Some dogs are less athletic than others and are less apt to jump up. Dogs who are more friendly to strangers than others, often as part of their breed heritage, are more inclined to have a jumping-up problem. I get the most complaints from owners of Golden and Labrador Retrievers. The combination of size, energy level, and overwhelming friendliness makes jumping up a challenging problem for owners of these dogs to correct.

Much of the training necessary for dealing with a jumping-up problem is detailed in Chapter 5. Start by perfecting the sit-stay for petting exercise from the basic training described in Week 1. Make sure your dog will consistently stay sitting when someone approaches him and pets him. This means he is doing it without being held in place with a tight leash or a death grip on his collar. He should be doing it in different places—at the door when company comes (as described in Week 4), outside in your yard, and when he meets people on walks.

While you are training him, it is a good idea to always have him on leash when people come to visit. Some people forget that leashes work just as well indoors as outdoors! Keep the leash close to the door so that it is handy when you need it. This makes it easy to correct him for jumping up, and you can then put him on a down-stay until he settles down. This is a necessity for an excitable dog. Some people may find it easier to keep their dogs under control when someone comes to the door by putting them on a down-stay. Keeping your dog down when someone comes in requires lots of persistent and patient practice, but think how impressed your company will be!

It is easy to get so involved with correcting your dog for jumping up that you forget to praise and reward him when he stays on the ground. This is a big mistake. Don't ignore him when he is patiently sitting in front of you. If the only time he gets your attention is when he jumps up, even though it is negative attention, he will keep jumping up. You must pet him and pay attention to him when he is not jumping up.

Once he is doing well at the sit-stay for petting on leash, it is time to progress in your training. Teach him to sit-stay for petting without the leash, and then try doing it with you standing a few feet away. Next work on the stand-stay for petting, as described in Weeks 4 and 5 of Chapter 5. Again, try to get your dog to do this off leash and with you a short distance away.

Consistency is essential for solving this problem. You cannot let your dog jump up sometimes and try to prevent him from doing so at others. This is a case where you need to discipline yourself, not your dog. You also cannot get away with skipping the basic training, so, as a famous dog training saying goes, "Train, don't complain."

It is important if you are going to teach your dog not to jump up on other people that you don't isolate him. Before he is trained, it will seem easier to just put him outside or in another room, but he will never have an opportunity to learn that way, and the isolation will probably make him more excited and more likely to jump in the future. In fact, the more people he meets, the less excited he will be when meeting someone and therefore the less likely he will be to jump up. Take him places where he can meet lots of people. A favorite of mine is outside the main building of a local college when classes are changing. Almost every student stops to say hello and pat the dog, and by the hundredth student, the dog is too tired to jump up. Then you can praise and reward him for his good behavior.

Jumping up is a particularly difficult problem when small children are involved. Start by training your dog not to chase the children in the first place. Practice having your dog do a sit-stay and down-stay while the kids race around. Also practice using the "Off" command with your dog on leash while the children jump around. Don't forget the praise!

Children over the age of four or five years can be taught to perform the come and sit exercise in order to encourage a dog to sit instead of jumping up on them. An adult should first teach the dog the exercise. Then the child should be taught how to get the dog to sit for food. Show the child how to make the hand motion to get your dog to sit and how to give a loud, firm command. If the child is young, hold his hand and guide it in the proper motion. Practice first without the dog. It will help if you tell the child to keep the piece of food closed in his fist, and not to open it and give it to the dog until you say to. He should open his hand flat to allow the dog to take the food. If he holds it in the tips of his fingers, he might get nibbled on and become frightened. It may be hard to overcome the child's natural tendency to jerk his hand away and try to hold it out of the dog's reach, but not doing so will just encourage the dog to jump more. An added advantage of working with a child on this exercise is that you are teaching your dog not to jump up and grab food out of a child's hand.

When the sitting is going well, add the come part. Again, teach the child how to give the proper command ("Max, come"). Then hold the dog a few feet away and release him when the child calls. The child should then give the sit command and hand signal. Practice calling the dog back and forth between you and the child.

A useful tool for working on a jumping-up problem is a spray bottle, like the kind used for misting plants. This should be filled with a solution of equal parts of distilled white vinegar and water. When your dog starts to jump up on you, give the "Off" command, then spray him in the face. The vinegar solution is more effective than plain water but will not damage his eyes, nor will it damage furniture or carpets. It is *very* important that you give the command first, and then use the spray bottle. If you spray him first, he will never learn to stay off on command and will only behave when you have the spray bottle with you. If jumping up is a particular problem when you come home from work in your good clothes and are faced with an excited dog, you might want to leave the spray bottle outside the door. The spray bottle correction is a good method because it will not provoke an aggressive response the way a physical correction might with some dogs.

The spray bottle is an especially good way for children to correct a dog because it does not involve any physical strength, but they must only be allowed to use it when directly supervised by an adult. The temptation to chase the dog around the house spraying him is too much for most children to resist. One client of mine found it useful in the mornings when the combination of a twelve-week-old Golden Retriever puppy fresh from a night of sleep and three boys between the ages of seven and twelve years rushing around to get off to school resulted in clothes being ripped and torn when the puppy jumped up to grab them. The boys used the spray bottle to discourage this bad habit.

There are probably times when you don't mind if your dog jumps up on you. Such enthusiastic expressions of love are hard to resist. Besides, it only seems fair to sometimes let him express himself in a way that is natural to him. It is okay to allow your dog to jump up on you when you invite him to do so. Establish a command or signal to let him know it is okay. You could just say "Okay," his release word, or pat your body, or make an upward signal with your arms. In fact, a good way to teach your dog the meaning of the word "off" is to alternate inviting him to jump up, then saying "Off" to get him to get down.

A marvelous example of using a special command for jumping up was taught by a friend of mine to her huge male Irish Wolfhound named Milo. Jumping up takes on a new meaning when one is talking about the tallest breed of dog. Milo puts his paws on my shoulders and has to *bend down* to lick my face. Milo's command to jump up is, appropriate enough, "Get tall." Milo is beautifully trained and never jumps up without his command. He loves to do this so much that his owner uses it as a reward for training. I recently ran into my friend and Milo at a dog show. We don't see each other often because we live

Milo, the Irish Wolfhound, "getting tall."

a distance apart, but Milo is always thrilled to see me. I kept him for a couple weeks as a favor to my friend when he was a very young puppy, so he regards me as his second mother. We couldn't let him "get tall" until I was done showing my dog and could suffer the damage to my clothes, so Milo impatiently waited for his command. When it finally came, I braced myself for receiving his 125 pounds and gave the command. The ensuing action attracted the attention of everyone in the vicinity, and Milo and I enjoyed expressing our deep affection for each other.

DESTRUCTIVE CHEWING

Let's get one thing straight from the start: Dogs do *not* destroy things out of spite. Most of the time they do so to relieve tension caused by stress. Just as people sometimes smoke, eat, drink, or take drugs to cope with tension, dogs chew. The solution lies in relieving your dog's tension and unhappiness, and, if that is not possible, in confining him to prevent further damage to your possessions and to himself.

Like all behavior problems, destructive chewing is affected by your dog's personality. Different things stress dogs with different personalities. If your dog is dependent, he will be stressed by being left alone. A high-energy dog is stressed by lack of exercise. A highly reactive dog is stressed by too much stimulation.

The most severe and repetitive cases of destructive chewing are caused by a problem called separation anxiety. This means that a dog becomes so anxious at being left alone and separated from his owner that he chews to relieve the tension. This kind of stress can be hard to alleviate, because you can't stay home with your dog all the time. Some things may help, such as giving your dog more exercise and leaving the radio on while you are gone so that the house isn't silent. It helps not to have emotional scenes whenever you leave and return. Some dogs do better if they have the company of another dog, or even a cat.

If none of these things work, you will have to confine your dog. Ways to confine your dog are discussed in Chapter 2 under the sections entitled "Confinement and Using a Crate" and "Confinement When You Work All Day." Confining a dog with separation anxiety in a small room may not work because some dogs will destroy the door and walls. These same dogs who are panic-stricken in a small room will often feel secure and safe in a crate.

You will notice that there is no mention of punishment for destructive chewing. The reason for this is illustrated by a story told in Chapter 1. Most punishment for destructive chewing is given hours after the chewing has taken place, as dogs are usually most upset right after their owners leave. The dog doesn't understand why he is being punished, although some owners mistakenly assume their dogs know because they behave in a submissive manner. The dog acts afraid because his owner is angry, *not* because he knows he has done something wrong. Not only does punishment not work, it can actually make

Dogs, like humans, may relieve tension by destructive behavior.

matters worse because it will make the dog more anxious and therefore more likely to chew in the future.

Some dogs with separation anxiety can tolerate the regular hours of separation that occur when their owners go to work, but are stressed if their owners leave them at unusual times, such as going out in the evening if they work during the day. Such dogs may need to be confined only during those unusual times.

Destructive chewing can also be caused by something happening outside the house that frustrates your dog, or even frightens him. The molding around a window can be destroyed because a car accident occurs outside the house while the owner is away and the dog is upset by all the commotion going on outside. If the chewing occurs near a door or window, look for something outside your house that is frustrating your dog. Are there squirrels playing outside where your dog can see them? Do a lot of people walk dogs by your house? Is your dog afraid of loud noises that frighten him when he is home alone? My Greyhound offers a good example. While she is not at all upset if I drive away from the house, she is terribly frustrated if I go out to my dog training building, which is just twenty feet from my back door. From my bedroom window she can see into the window in the door of the building and catching glimpses of me as I move about. Her reaction is to grab a magazine lying on the nightstand and tear it to shreds. There are magazines lying all over the house in all sorts of accessible places, but these are the only magazines she ever touches. At first I had to crate her at these times, but now I only have to shut the bedroom door. If this kind of frustration is causing your dog's destruction problem, either change what is happening outside or restrict your dog's ability to see outside.

Dogs may chew out of boredom. The best remedy for this is to alleviate your dog's boredom. Get him out of the house. Take him places with you. Find him a dog friend to play with once in a while. Enroll him in a dog obedience class. Teach him some tricks to entertain your friends and family. He will love the attention these get. Destructive chewing may also be caused by lack of exercise or the tension caused by family conflict.

Puppies chew out of curiosity and playfulness. Because of their tendency to get into things that may hurt them, puppies should be safely confined when you are gone. Once they get older, you can try giving them some freedom when you are away on a short errand. Your dog may be one to two years old before this is possible.

I will include a few words about dogs getting into trash and stealing food from counters when you are gone. Put the trash can someplace where your dog can't reach it, and put the food out of the dog's reach. Such items offer too much temptation to a dog. These acts can be more easily solved by prevention than by training. These behavior problems, along with destructive chewing, all fall into the category of owner-absent problems. Some dogs are so easily inhibited that once they are punished by their owner, they never repeat the behavior, even when their owner is gone. Other dogs figure out that they won't be punished when their owner is absent. Punishment won't help train these dogs. You are better off making changes that prevent the dog from getting into trouble.

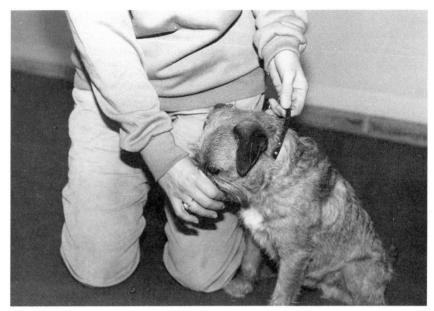

You can stop a dog's barking by pushing down on his muzzle while pulling up on his collar.

Using a spray bottle to correct barking. (Border Terrier)

Dogs sometimes chew simply because they like to chew. They like to gnaw on something hard and to shred things into little pieces (causing the demise of many chair legs and foam pillows). Make sure your dog has plenty of safe things to chew on. Mine seem to get a lot of satisfaction from something as simple as ripping apart an empty ice cream carton. If you have any doubt about the safety of something you want to give your dog, such as rawhide bones, check with your veterinarian.

EXCESSIVE BARKING

It is interesting that wolves rarely bark, while dogs often do. Of course, wolves do not have cats walking outside a fence just beyond their reach, nor do they have mailmen trespassing onto their territory on a daily basis. Barking seems to be a behavior born of the many frustrations experienced by dogs living in a domestic setting. Excessive barking is often a prelude to biting, so it is a problem to be taken seriously.

Many people are initially reluctant to correct their dog for barking because they appreciate the protection that barking affords. The security of having a dog that barks to warn you of intruders is desirable, but this barking should not be allowed to get out of control. What you want is for your dog only to bark at appropriate things, and then to stop barking on your command.

First of all, decide what you want your dog to bark at and correct him for barking at anything else. For instance, a small child going by your house on a bicycle hardly poses a threat and should not be barked at. However, barking at a delivery man driving up your driveway is okay. Dogs that live in apartments should only bark when someone knocks on the door.

Then teach your dog to stop barking on your command. The command I use is "That's enough." Stopping the barking can be difficult. Start by calmly going to your dog and taking hold of his collar. If the barking was appropriate, praise him with a quiet "Good boy." Then say "That's enough." If he doesn't stop, give him a firm shake with the collar, repeating "That's enough." You can also try grabbing his muzzle with your right hand and pushing it down while you pull up on his collar with the left hand. The second he stops barking, *praise*. You could even give him a food reward. He may resume barking immediately. Repeat the command and correction until he stops.

If your dog's barking has reached the point of hysteria, you might want to try the spray bottle technique described above in the section on jumping up. As before, fill it with a fifty-fifty mixture of distilled white vinegar and water. Give the command to stop barking, then spray him in the face. He is bound to stop, if only for a millisecond, but be sure to praise when he does.

By teaching your dog to stop barking on command, you are preventing the barking from escalating to biting. Many people do not see the relationship between barking and biting and are surprised when their out-of-control barkers bite someone. The purpose of barking is to warn off intruders; if that doesn't work, biting is sometimes the next step the dog will take.

To keep barking under control, every time your dog barks you must go check it out, praise him for barking if it was appropriate, and then tell him to stop.

If your dog is barking when he is outside, either in a fenced yard or on a chain, he is doing so because he is frustrated. The best way to solve the problem is to reduce your dog's frustration. The easiest way may be to simply keep your dog inside and only allow him out when you are with him or for short periods of time, not long enough to become bored and frustrated. You can also change the environment somehow, with plants, privacy fencing, or vinyl strips woven into the fencing to reduce the visibility of whatever causes your dog's frustration and barking. If he barks when he is outside with you, correct the same way you would if he were inside. Do not allow the frustration to build, especially if the barking is at people or children, because the dog may eventually bite in frustration.

If the reason your dog is frustrated and barking is that he is isolated in the backyard, solve the problem that caused you to isolate him in the first place so that he can have some much needed companionship.

SHYNESS

Shyness, or fear of people, is a serious problem because if a dog becomes fearful enough, he may bite. This problem is commonly referred to as fear biting. If you see shyness in a puppy, even if he is as young as five weeks, don't count on him growing out of it and start working on it right away. In less severe cases of shyness, good training can almost completely make the problem disappear. For instance, as I indicated in Chapter 1, my first dog, an Irish Setter, was shy. We struggled in our first obedience class trying to persuade her to allow the instructor to touch her. After being obedience trained, no one would believe that she was ever shy. She visited nursing homes and schools regularly to put on obedience demonstrations, always allowing everyone to pet her afterward. More severe cases of shyness respond less dramatically to training, but usually there is some improvement.

Shyness can either be genetic or caused by a lack of socialization when the dog is a puppy. The hereditary version can be found in all pure-breds as well as mixed breeds. The widespread nature of this problem is understandable if you look at the heritage of the dog before it was domesticated. Wolves, a close relative of the dog, are timid and shy by nature. This is a helpful adaptation for their survival. Domestication has reduced this shyness in dogs, but the trait can still be present in their genes and can often appear when dogs are bred indiscriminately. An inherited shyness problem can be improved greatly with training, but it cannot be totally erased.

The other cause of shyness is a lack of socialization. Dogs that do not receive adequate human contact between the ages of five and twelve weeks are usually shy of humans. This can happen when puppies are raised outside in a barn or kennel, or in a puppy mill situation. This shyness can also be improved with training, but you can never completely compensate for the lack of socialization. Shyness of strange people and places can also occur if a puppy is only exposed to the people who own him and the place where he lives until the age of sixteen weeks.

When people get shy dogs from animal shelters, they often assume that it is the result of previous abuse. While abuse can cause shyness, such shyness quickly fades when the dog is placed in a loving, understanding, consistent environment. If shyness persists in such dogs, it is probably a congenital problem, not the result of abuse. Dogs also do not become permanently shy from one traumatic incident, such as being roughly handled by a veterinarian or groomer. A dog with a good, stable temperament cannot be changed into a shy dog with one incident.

Some dogs also exhibit shyness when they enter their adolescence, somewhere around the age of six to nine months, even though they have never shown any previous shyness problems. The stress of hormonal changes probably has something to do with this. Treat this type as you would any other form of shyness, but be especially careful to avoid forcing your dog into a situation that is too stressful for him to handle. By doing so you could turn a temporary problem into a permanent one.

No matter what the cause of shyness, an obedience training class is a great help. (See Chapter 10 for how to find a good class.) Try to find a class taught by someone experienced in handling shy dogs. By going to a class, a shy dog gets to meet people and other dogs in a strange place but in a controlled situation. He gets to see the same people and dogs every week, which helps him to become gradually less frightened. Being told specifically what to do and how to behave also helps him cope with a frightening situation. The praise and treats he will get as he learns will make him feel good about himself. He will learn to tolerate the instructor petting him while he is made to stay. In many ways, a class can be a confidence-building experience for a shy dog.

The two most important tools in dealing with a shy dog are food and the sit-stay. You will use the food to encourage him to approach people he is afraid of, and the sit-stay to prevent your dog from backing away from a stranger.

Start working on your shyness problem by using food at whatever level your dog is comfortable. Shy dogs are more comfortable approaching someone on their own than being approached, so you want to start by teaching your dog to approach people to get a treat. If your dog is so afraid that he will not approach a person to take food from their hand, start by having that person sit on the floor and toss food to the dog, gradually decreasing the distance that the food is thrown until the dog is taking a piece of food from the person's hand outstretched at arm's length.

Continue training your dog by encouraging him to approach people offering him food. *Don't forget to praise him whenever he acts in a friendly, confident manner.* When he will readily approach someone holding out a piece of food, start having people do the approaching while your dog is on a sit-stay.

Take advantage of any and every opportunity to have someone strange feed your dog. Carry treats with you when you go for walks to hand to people. You

Offering a shy dog food will help him overcome his fear of people.   (Mixed breed)

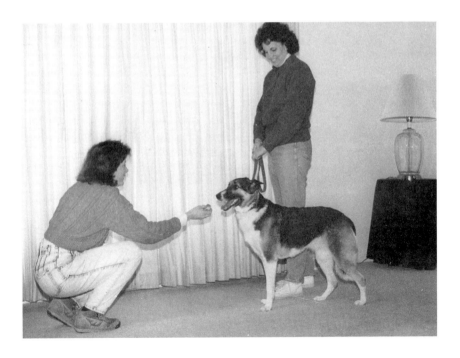

want your dog to think that everyone he meets is a potential source of treats, rather than a threat.

It is critical in dealing with this problem not to unintentionally reward your dog for acting shy and make the problem worse. When your dog is afraid of someone, it is natural to try to reassure him. However, he has no way of understanding that your reassurance is regarding the person. Instead, he will think your soft words and petting are an expression of approval for his fearful behavior. This is certainly not what you want to teach him. An example of this is given in Chapter 3 in ''Building Confidence.''

What you want to communicate to your dog instead is that he is acting silly and that you are not going to tolerate it. Speak firmly to him in a no-nonsense tone of voice. If he is a little dog, do not pick him up and cuddle him. Don't let him lean on you or hide behind you. Rather, place him on a sit-stay on your left side and stubbornly make him stay there. If the most he can tolerate at first is a person walking around him in a circle, staying ten feet away, start there. Then gradually work up to having him sit and stay while an unfamiliar person approaches him and hands him a piece of food. When your dog is comfortable with this, make him do a sit-stay while the person approaches and pets him *before* giving him the food reward. You will know you really have your problem under control when you can leave your dog on a sit-stay, go six feet away, and have a stranger pet your dog without you standing right next to him for security.

You will need to get your shy dog out and exposed to people and places. Be very careful when you do so that you do not put your dog in a situation that makes him so afraid that he feels forced to bite to defend himself. Watch your dog carefully for any signs that he is feeling uncomfortable and remove him from the situation before he becomes frightened. While shy dogs need to be pushed to face their fears, there is a point at which you can stress them too much and cause them to become more fearful. It is important to read your dog so that you know when to stop. Watch the expression in his eyes as well as the tenseness of his muscles. If he refuses to eat his treats, that is a sign that he is stressed.

If your dog's shyness or fear causes him to growl or bite, please see the next chapter on aggression.

One final thought: Do not breed from a shy dog. It is impossible to know for sure if a dog is shy because of a genetic problem that he or she can pass on to offspring or if this condition was caused by a lack of socialization. There is no way to go back and see if your dog would have had a good temperament if he had received adequate socialization. And please do not use the excuse that your dog is shy because of a traumatic incident to justify breeding a shy dog. It is irresponsible to take a chance on producing another generation of shy puppies when the world is grievously overpopulated with dogs.

9

Aggression

PEOPLE NEVER CALL ME and say that they have a biting problem with their dog. Instead, the usual phone call goes something like this:

OWNER: Hello. I think my dog needs some training.
ME: What problems are you having?
OWNER: Well, he doesn't like some people.
ME: What do you mean by not liking people?
OWNER: He just doesn't like some people.

(By now I guess that there is a problem the owner is having trouble admitting to, and that getting information is going to be like pulling teeth.)

ME: Has he ever bitten anyone?
OWNER: Well, he once snapped at a man he didn't like.
ME: Did he bite the man?
OWNER: Well, sort of.
ME: Was the skin broken?
OWNER: Yes.
ME: Did it require stitches?
OWNER: Yes, a few.
ME: How many?
OWNER: Well, ten, but this is the only person he's bitten that had to go to the hospital. He's really a nice dog most of the time.

You may laugh, but I am not exaggerating. One of the most dangerous things about dog aggression problems is that people often deny that the problem exists until it is fairly advanced and therefore harder to solve or, even worse, until someone is badly bitten. The purpose of this chapter is to help you recognize if your dog has an aggression problem and to help you understand it. It is *not* about how you can solve your dog's aggression problem. Diagnosing and solving this kind of problem, if it can be solved, generally requires expert help.

There are many reasons why people might deny that their dog has an aggression problem. Many people like their dog's protectiveness until it gets out of control and becomes a liability. Some owners blame their dog's aggression on abuse the dog might have suffered before he came to live with them, and they hope that love will cure it. Others think it is just puppy behavior and that their dog will grow out of it as he matures. People may put off seeking help because it is hard to admit that they are afraid of their dog. A common excuse is to blame the victim for provoking the dog, even if the provocation was a nonthreatening act, such as petting the dog.

"But he's nice most of the time." This is a statement I often hear when dog owners contact me about their dog's aggression problem, and it explains why it is hard for owners to face their dog's problem. Their dogs *are* affectionate, cute, and playful some of the time, with some people. The owners love their dogs. The incidents of aggressive behavior occur infrequently at first, so it is easy to make excuses for a few nasty encounters until someone gets hurt. Oftentimes the owners don't even realize that they are learning what to do to avoid "setting the dog off" and they deceive themselves into thinking that he is getting better.

Biting, snapping, and growling are behaviors that can have many different causes. A dog may snap and growl as a form of play, or he may do it because he has some form of brain damage. Understanding the cause of aggressive behavior is important in deciding how to handle it. Here is a partial list of things that may cause aggressive behavior toward humans:

- fear (which can be caused by many things)
- protection of territory
- possessiveness of an object
- protection of a litter of puppies
- psychosis
- abuse
- pain
- objection to being restrained
- interpreting punishment as an attack
- a drug side effect
- being raised without littermates or without a mother to teach inhibition of aggression.

Because a dog cannot talk and tell you why he is biting, determining the cause requires good detective work: adding together the clues given by the dog's body language and behavior, asking the right questions about the dog's behavior, obtaining a thorough history of the dog's problem and upbringing, and looking at the dog's breeding. While an expert is best at preparing such a profile, this chapter should help you start to understand dog aggression problems.

Although some general patterns will be described, aggression problems cannot be easily categorized. All dogs are individuals with different backgrounds, both genetically and environmentally, that affect the problem. No two aggression problems are exactly alike. To complicate the situation, a dog may have more than one kind of aggression problem. Aggression against humans and aggression directed at other dogs are two separate problems, although both may exist in one dog.

The first and major part of this chapter will concentrate on aggression against humans, because as an obedience instructor I receive more complaints about this kind of aggression. Aggression with other dogs is a less common complaint; this will be briefly discussed at the end of the chapter.

Keep in mind as you read about aggression that the really remarkable thing about dogs in general is not how aggressive they can be, but how gentle and willing to inhibit their bites they are.

DOG PERSONALITY TYPES AND AGGRESSION

Almost any dog will bite if stressed severely enough, but dogs with some personality types are more likely to bite than others. Among the personality factors that increase the likelihood that a dog will bite are breed predisposition, aggressive defense reactions, assertiveness, and excitability (see Chapter 4 for more about these personality factors).

Some breeds were developed to bite and behave aggressively as part of their job. These include the herding breeds, terriers, and guarding breeds. Other breeds have had aggressive tendencies purposely bred out of them. For instance, I rarely see biting problems in Golden Retrievers and Siberian Huskies; aggression would be detrimental to both of these breeds' work patterns. Knowing your breed's aggression potential can alert you to early signs of an aggression problem so that it can be better managed. Since Lhasa Apsos may seem like lapdogs and Dalmatians like spotted clowns, ignorance of the protective behavior bred into these breeds may lead owners to overlook problems until someone is bitten. Of course, these are generalizations, and there is much variation among individuals within a breed.

As noted in Chapter 4, some dogs will respond to stress, especially when frightened or cornered, by biting, while others will remain passive. Such aggressive defense reactions can become worse as a dog learns that they do indeed provide a good defense. Whenever dealing with dogs of this personality type, avoid confrontations that may cause the dog to bite. You don't want to give him the opportunity to learn the effectiveness of biting.

A dog with aggressive defense reactions may respond to punishment by growling or biting. He may interpret some kinds of punishment as an attack against which he has to defend himself. If so, change the punishment, or eliminate it. Any punishment in which anger is an overriding emotion, or lasts more than a few seconds, not to mention punishment that takes the form more of a beating than a reprimand, is likely to be misunderstood by a dog.

The assertive dog may let you know he is annoyed by something with a growl or bite. This can be seen in a seven-week-old puppy. There is no need to panic. It doesn't mean you have a vicious dog. It does mean you have to control this tendency. Your dog has the right to express himself, but he does not have the right to escalate that expression into greater aggression. If you bother your dog by petting him when he is exhausted and trying to sleep, and he growls to let you know it, there is no need for punishment. But take note of such a reaction, and make sure he will let you handle him when you have to. If the assertive aggressiveness of an adolescent male dog with his increased levels of testosterone becomes a problem, he will benefit from neutering. The resultant reduction in sexual tension will help him relax.

A dog that is excitable, or highly reactive to stimulation, may or may not have a tendency to bite. They are two separate characteristics. A dog may be very difficult to provoke, because he is not excitable, but when he finally is sufficiently provoked he will respond by biting. This would be typical of some large, heavy-boned member of the guard breeds. On the other hand, a very excitable Labrador Retriever may never defend himself by biting, no matter how much he is provoked. However, an excitable dog with aggressive tendencies, such as a nervous German Shepherd who is quick to snap, can be dangerous if not carefully supervised.

While personality factors are inherited and hard to change, early recognition of aggressive tendencies and appropriate training can prevent aggression problems from developing.

DOES YOUR DOG HAVE AN AGGRESSION PROBLEM?

The first step in dealing with your dog's aggression problem is deciding whether or not he has one. This is confusing because some aggression is considered acceptable and even desirable in dogs. In fact, probably an important reason why the dog was domesticated was their instinctive ability to warn their human owners of intruders and drive the intruders away. Guarding has always been a valued characteristic of dogs.

In deciding if your dog has an aggression problem, it is not a question of what is normal or natural aggression for a dog, but what is acceptable to the human society in which dogs live. In most cases, the only legally and socially acceptable provocations for biting that relieve an owner of liability are illegal trespassing on the dog owner's property; attacking the owner; or kicking, teasing, or in some other way tormenting the dog. While it may be natural for a dog to want to drive away all strangers that come into his territory, or to defend himself against the man in the white coat who attacks him with needles and thermometers, such behaviors cause problems in the dog-human relationship.

The following is a list of signals that your dog may have an aggression problem. If your answer is yes to any of these questions, you should seek help.

1. Has your dog ever snapped at or bitten anyone except under circumstances involving the provocations listed above?
2. Has your dog ever growled or snapped at you when you tried to discipline him?
3. Has your dog ever growled or snapped at you when you tried to take something away from him?
4. Do you avoid touching your dog in certain ways because you are afraid you will irritate him?
5. Does your dog snap at you when you try to brush him?
6. Has a groomer complained to you about having difficulty handling your dog?
7. Has your dog tried to snap at your veterinarian?
8. Does your dog bark hysterically when someone either comes to the house or goes by your house? Can you easily stop your dog from barking in these situations?
9. Does your dog growl at people after they enter your home, continue barking at them, or shy away from them?
10. Does your dog shy away from strangers when they try to touch him?
11. Do you not trust your dog around strangers?
12. Do you find yourself making excuses for your dog's hostile behavior?
13. Is your dog less than six months old and already acting hostile toward strangers?

Some signs are harder to see than others, but no matter what the signs are, you can always make excuses. Don't deny an aggression problem.

FEAR AGGRESSION

Fear, whether caused by a lack of socialization or a genetic shyness, can cause a dog to bite. It is the aggression problem I see most frequently. Shyness is a common temperament problem in dogs, and people often inadvertently make the shyness worse by unintentionally rewarding their dog for shy behavior, as was described in Chapter 3 in the section about building confidence in a dog. Such rewarding can turn shyness into fear biting.

Fear aggression can progress to the point where a dog will attack to prevent an approach. Because the dog is initiating the attack, it is hard to see the fear behind it. Since looking at a dog usually precedes an approach, some dogs will attack when eye contact is made. I once worked with a dog who would growl if you made eye contact with him when he was thirty feet away. He put on quite a ferocious display if you approached closer. One time, in the middle of an aggressive lunge, his leash snapped. It was apparent that these attacks were meant to drive people away rather than attack them because he almost stopped in midair and ran back to hug his owner's side. Such behavior always reminds me of the Cowardly Lion in *The Wizard of Oz*. This is the best way to tell if the

Whenever a dog shows fear in his body language, owners should be aware of the potential for dog bites. (German Shepherd)

Attempting to reassure a dog who is afraid may unintentionally reward aggressive behavior.

171

aggression you are seeing in a dog is based on fear. When a dog with this problem lunges forward to snap at someone, he quickly withdraws.

Treating fear aggression starts by treating the underlying shyness. Some techniques for this were described in Chapter 8 in "Shyness."

As important as treating the dog with fear aggression problems is treating the owner. The behavior patterns and attitudes of the owner have to be changed. The owner must stop feeling sorry for his dog, or at least expressing it, because this will only make his dog worse. He has to stop making excuses ("Poor Whiskers has never liked men"). All unintentional rewarding as the owner attempts to reassure his dog must be stopped. Instead, the owner must take a tougher line. No longer will growling, barking, backing away, or acting nervous be tolerated. He must encourage his dog to face the things that make him afraid and learn that they are not a threat. He must also correct his dog for all signs of aggression, telling him firmly "no" and giving him a collar correction. The proper time to give this correction is when the dog starts to growl. The owner must clearly communicate his dislike of such fearful and aggressive behavior.

A common mistake is to misinterpret fear biting as "over-protectiveness." The typical scenario is a dog pressed close against his owner, growling and baring his teeth at someone approaching, while the owner attempts to soothe the dog. The owner thinks the dog is protecting her, when in reality the dog is hoping the owner will protect him! Meanwhile, the owner's attempts to reassure her dog only serve to reward him for his aggressive behavior. The problem gets worse, until the dog darts forward and nips someone. The belief in the dog's "protectiveness" is reinforced by the fact that the dog displays the most or sometimes the only aggression when he is with his owner—not because he is protecting his owner, but because his owner's support gives him the false courage he needs to attack. In this situation, the owner's attitude is often the hardest problem to correct, because the idea of being protected by one's dog is so gratifying. The owner may make halfhearted attempts to correct his dog, but the dog will interpret his owner's body language and will know what the real story is.

RESTRAINT AGGRESSION

Because a dog's natural inclination is to flee from something he is afraid of rather than fight, tremendous stress is put on a dog when he is frightened and cannot escape. That is why dogs often bite when they are restrained. Dogs must be taught to accept the restraint that is necessary in domesticated life. This is more difficult with dogs of some personality traits than with others. An excitable dog with aggressive defense reactions and an assertive personality will obviously be harder to train in this regard than a passive dog, who may require no training at all. This aggression often shows up when a dog tries to bite the veterinarian or someone grooming him. If your veterinarian or groomer must muzzle your dog or tranquilize him, you have a problem.

Some groomers in my area will refer dogs to me that they find too aggressive to handle. That is how I came to meet Dundee, a mixed breed with a long, shaggy coat. Dundee's coat was so matted that his skin was becoming infected. He was a pleasant, playful dog until he saw someone approaching with a brush. If unable to escape, he launched into a frightening attack against that person. When he was little, he had snapped one time when his owner was brushing him. She then became afraid of brushing him. Of course, the more matted he got, the more it hurt when his owner tried to brush him, so he became more aggressive.

We started working on Dundee's problem by teaching him to lie down with food, since this would be the position in which we eventually wanted to brush him. At the same time, Dundee's owner placed the scissors and brush next to his food bowl for a week when she fed him. While we continued to teach him to accept restraint, using liberal food rewards, we enticed him to come to us when we were holding the brush by offering him food.

Our next step was to have him lie down on his side while we waved the scissors and brush over him, without touching him. We continued this until he accepted it without showing signs of panic. Again, food rewards flowed freely.

Finally, we were ready to attempt cutting out the mats. Dundee's coat was too matted to be brushed. It would have been just too painful for him, and he didn't need his fears reinforced by unnecessary pain. We managed to clip a few mats before he started showing signs of stress. We released him from his down-stay and rewarded him. He looked moth-eaten when he left, with big chunks missing from his coat, but his owner and I were jubilant at our success.

A different type of restraint problem occurs when a dog reacts aggressively to being grabbed by the collar. This can be caused by someone grabbing the dog to physically punish him, or it may simply be a case of an assertive dog that just doesn't like being prevented from doing what he wants. First, all grabbing of the dog must be stopped. Then the dog can be taught using the come and sit exercise in Chapter 5 that includes grabbing the collar. You want to have your dog associate having his collar grabbed with receiving food rewards. Training is also the answer for the assertive dog.

FAMILY CONFLICT AND AGGRESSION

Unfortunately, from time to time I see dog bites that are the result of hostility among the human members of a household. This happens most often in response to fighting by a married couple. A dog can be horribly stressed by such fighting and may bite because of the stress. In this case, the biting may occur in any situation that is already somewhat stressful for the dog, such as while guarding a rawhide bone or while strangers are visiting. Dogs may also direct their stress-related aggression at a child or another dog.

Another situation with potential for a dog bite is when the dog "takes sides" in the fighting and attacks one of the people involved. Dogs may bite in any situation that stresses them and from which there is no escape, and family conflict is no exception.

While barking a warning is a trait most dog owners welcome, allowing territorial aggression to get out of control can lead to problems. (Belgian Tervuren)

PROTECTIVE AGGRESSION

As mentioned in an earlier part of this chapter, the trait of territorial protective aggression has been valued in dogs since their domestication and selectively bred for. This trait varies tremendously in dogs, from dogs that show absolutely no protectiveness to others that gladly attack to defend their territory and try to keep enlarging the territory they defend.

The development of territorial protectiveness in dogs is linked to sexual maturity. A dog is most easily guided into appropriate but not excessive protective behavior if the protectiveness is addressed at the time it first appears. Owners of protective dogs have a responsibility to teach their dogs the limits of their protectiveness. Don't be reticent about putting limits on your dog's protectiveness for fear that he will cease all protection. You want to teach him what you consider threatening and what you do not. You also want to teach him that when you are home you will make the decision about who is permitted in your house and who is not.

As described in Chapter 8, barking problems are warnings of territorial protection problems. By controlling a dog's excessive barking, the owner takes the first step toward solving a territorial protection problem.

It is important to note that if you think you are seeing protectiveness in a dog of less than six months of age, it is likely that what you really are seeing is fear aggression. One way to differentiate fear aggression from protective aggression is to evaluate the dog's response in various settings. The protective dog is friendly to strangers when out of his territory, even though he is accompanied by his owner. The fearful dog behaves aggressively toward strangers anywhere.

Another mistake that people make with regard to protectiveness is the myth perpetuated by television and literature that dogs naturally protect their owners. Dogs will instinctively protect their territory, mostly preferring to drive intruders away rather than engage in a confrontation. They will protect themselves and their food and toys, but they rarely protect people, with the exception of when a child becomes a puppy substitute and is protected by a dog. Dogs are trained to attack people (and note that training is required to get a dog with a good temperament to attack people) by forcing the dog to attack to defend himself, or by making use of his instinct to kill prey.

The perfect guard dog is one who is confident around people and not afraid of them. In fact, he is very friendly with people. He barks when someone strange comes onto your property, but ignores children riding by on bicycles. He stops barking on your command, but continues to keep a watchful eye. If you say someone at your door is okay, he willingly makes friendly overtures to them. He would not allow anyone to enter your house when you are not home except for a few friends or family members he knows well. You feel secure when you are alone at home that you will be alerted if someone arrives, yet you are never afraid that your dog will bite someone when you have company. Because he is not afraid of people, if he ever does have to defend his territory, he won't hesitate. This kind of dog is the product of the right breed, good breeding, and good training.

A WORD ABOUT ATTACK-TRAINED DOGS

Although I don't remember where I read it, I remember another dog trainer making a very good point about the general public owning dogs trained to attack. He (or she) said that since most people cannot reliably make their dogs sit and stay, the idea of such people owning a dog trained to attack is frightening. If you feel that your home needs more protection, buy a burglar alarm. It is more reliable, and it won't attack the wrong person.

PSYCHOTIC AGGRESSIVE BEHAVIOR

Psychotic aggressive behavior is aggression caused by a mental disorder. Psychosis is not well understood in humans, so it is not surprising that it is even less understood in dogs. Increasingly, physiological bases are being found for such problems in humans. It may be that there is a canine equivalent of paranoid schizophrenia, a psychotic disease known in humans to be caused by chemical imbalances in the brain. Sometimes this kind of aggressive behavior is seen in a puppy; more often, it appears or gets worse as the puppy matures into an adolescent. *Rage syndrome* is a term sometimes used to describe this behavior in dogs.

Psychotic aggressive behavior is characterized by the random nature of aggression. It is often directed at some family members but not others, with no apparent reason. While a trigger for the attack can sometimes be identified, there is usually no reason for the dog to feel threatened. Prior to attacking, the dog often exhibits rigid muscles and a fixed stare. Usually there is no growling or barking prior to the attack. The problem seems to appear more often in male dogs; castration does not help.

The combination of psychotic aggression with other forms of aggression, such as fear aggression and/or protective aggression, makes the diagnosis of this problem difficult. Psychotic aggressive behavior is sometimes difficult to distinguish from severe fear aggression. Fear aggression is not directed at family members, while psychotic aggression often is. Also, the ferocity of the attack is a clue, as fear biters just make quick nips and withdraw, while the psychotic aggressive dog makes a more unrestrained attack.

A Basset Hound I once evaluated is an example of the grief this problem brings to the owners of such dogs. The dog had been obtained as an adult dog to be the pet of a nine-year-old boy who had begged for a dog for years. When I visited the house, two of the three children were shut in their bedrooms for their own safety. The younger brother couldn't get near the dog, because he attacked him on sight with an unbelievable ferocity. In order for one of them to go to the bathroom, someone who could handle the dog had to shut him in another room in the house. This dog had completely disrupted the family. Fighting had broken out among the family members because everyone blamed someone else in the family for the dog's behavior.

Even though this dog was only two years old, this was his fourth home. This should have been a warning signal. When dogs have had several homes, it can be a sign of a temperament problem. The previous owners had given no warning of any problems. I am sure this problem existed previously, but the other owners avoided dealing with the problem by simply giving the dog away. This family had also been misled by their mistaken belief that the AKC papers that accompanied the Basset were evidence of quality. Examination of this dog's pedigree revealed that he was inbred, the result of a mother-son mating. I have seen such behavior in inbred dogs before. Inbreeding can bring out recessive genes that are probably the cause of psychotic behavior in some dogs. I recommended euthanasia for this dog and directed the family to a reputable Basset Hound breeder. I must emphasize that this behavior is not typical of Basset Hounds, and can be found in various breeds.

Earlier in my career as a dog trainer, I tried to train these dogs. Working with the owners, I was able to make an improvement in the dog's behavior. In all cases, however, checking with these owners after a year had passed revealed that the dog had bitten again. The incidents were always described as occurring without warning or provocation. In two cases, children were bitten badly enough to have to go to the hospital. I learned through experience that training does not cure this problem; it only covers it up and gives the owners a dangerously false sense of security. After careful evaluation to determine that this is indeed the type of aggression problem that has been presented to me, I no longer attempt to train these dogs and recommend euthanasia because of the dangers such dogs pose to the people around them.

DOGS AGGRESSIVE WITH OTHER DOGS

Just as there are many causes for aggression among humans, there are also many causes for aggression among dogs. The most common are aggression among males and a lack of socialization with other dogs.

As male dogs reach sexual maturity, their behavior is influenced by increased levels of the male hormone testosterone. This can cause some male dogs to become aggressive with other males. This can happen no matter how much socialization with other dogs your dog has received as a puppy. There seems to be some hereditary tendency with this problem. How aggressive an uncastrated male dog becomes can vary greatly. If there is room for the dogs to separate, the fights usually end with little or no physical damage done to either dog. Castrating your dog is the best solution if this aggression becomes a problem, although the older your dog is when it is done, the less effect it has. This problem is particularly difficult to handle when it involves two male dogs in the same household, since they cannot get away from each other. Often the only fair solution to the dogs is to find another home for one of them.

Dogs who lack socialization with other dogs, and especially dogs who were removed from their litter before the age of six weeks, do not know how to interact with other dogs, are often afraid of them, and consequently can become aggressive. Depending on how early in life this isolation from other dogs occurred, a dog with this problem may benefit from playing with a mild-mannered, gentle, nonthreatening dog. He may learn to feel comfortable with a few dogs he knows well, but not all dogs.

Another less common cause of aggression among dogs is predatory aggression. This is a misdirected version of the instinct that made it possible for dogs' ancestors to survive by hunting. Dogs with this problem see other dogs as prey. An unfortunate case of this was brought to me by someone whose Doberman Pinscher was attacking his other dog, an Australian Shepherd. It initially appeared to be a case of intermale aggression, since both were sexually mature male dogs who were not castrated. Clues that it went beyond this were that the Doberman attacked without warning growls or the body postures that characteristically precede intermale aggression. Another clue was that his attacks on the other dog consisted of biting in the neck area and attempting to pick up the Aussie and shake him. The Dobe badly wounded the Aussie before they were separated. Further investigation revealed that this Dobe would also attack female dogs and other animals when he managed to jump his fence. This Dobe was very friendly to people, including strangers, even though he had received brutal enough training by another trainer to put scars on his neck.

All these forms of dog-oriented aggression can be controlled but not totally eliminated by training. A dog with these problems can be taught to pay more attention to his owner than to other dogs, and the aggressive behavior can be corrected. However, it will probably not be possible to make the dog friendly with all dogs.

FINDING HELP

If you think your dog has an aggression problem, you need to get expert help, but it probably won't be easy to find. Anyone can call himself an animal behavior consultant or dog psychologist. There are no licensing requirements. This is complicated by the fact that someone with a Ph.D. in animal behavior may have little practical experience in handling aggressive dogs, while a dog trainer with no academic degrees may have a lot of experience and be of great help.

You can ask a veterinarian for referrals; however be cautious about taking your veterinarian's advice regarding your dog's aggression problem unless he has had special training in this area beyond the normal veterinary training. His advice may be well meaning but lacking a foundation in experience and knowledge. You could also contact the nearest veterinary school for a referral. They often have a dog behavior specialist on staff.

Taking an obedience class might be helpful if your aggression problem has not progressed far and if your dog is young. If you sign up for a class, tell the instructor about your aggression problem beforehand. Be honest with him or her.

The instructor may not feel qualified to handle your problem, or may feel that the class setting is inappropriate for your dog. He or she may require that you take some private lessons before entering a class.

When dealing with an aggression problem, don't add tension to tension, or aggression to aggression. If your dog is tense and in a situation in which you think he may bite, you will only increase the likelihood of that happening if you become tense yourself. Your dog will sense your fears and become more stressed himself, feeling more of a need to defend himself. Instead, try relaxing your dog with happy talk, play, and laughter. Don't increase your dog's aggression by adding aggression with punishment that is hostile in nature, excessive, and beyond the point of instructional correction.

CONCLUSION

This chapter has been a simplified overview of a very complex problem, and has only touched on the more common kinds of aggression problems. As previously mentioned, all dogs are individuals, making every aggression problem different and not easily categorized.

If your dog has an aggression problem, don't ignore it. Don't ignore the warning signals, and don't make excuses. Without help, it will probably get worse. Dogs learn that biting works; it drives away the source of their stress. Once a dog bites, he is more likely to bite again.

There are legal concerns in owning an aggressive dog. Society is increasingly intolerant of any nuisance created by dogs, and dog bites in particular are receiving a lot of publicity. New laws are being passed that emphasize the owner's liability for his dog's actions.

But more important than the legal concerns are the moral concerns. No one should have to suffer the pain and emotional trauma of a dog bite or attack. The emotional and physical effects can last a lifetime. Since dogs are everywhere in our society, a fear of dogs created by an attack can be a real handicap.

When it comes to aggression, it is the dog who ultimately pays for human error. Often he is the recipient of severe physical punishment before being finally euthanized. The key to prevention is careful breeding for good temperament and good training.

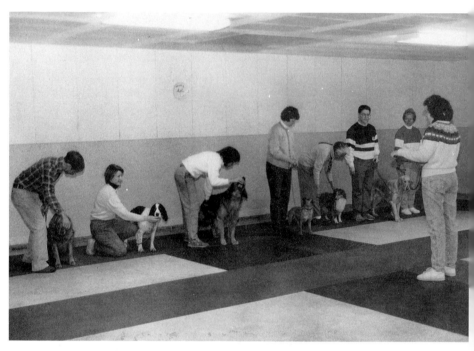

Participating in an obedience class can be beneficial and fun.

10

Great Adventures with Your Dog

THERE ARE MANY FUN THINGS you can do with your dog, especially once he has some basic training. This chapter will give you some suggestions. Besides being fun, the activities in this chapter provide your dog with the mental stimulation he needs to be happy. Dogs need more than physical exercise. They need mental exercise, too. They are intelligent, thinking beings who enjoy new experiences. And not only your dog will get mental stimulation. You will learn a lot, too.

Dog activities also provide a unique opportunity to meet new people. There is something about dogs that makes it easy to start a conversation with a stranger. Maybe it is because you don't have to start off by talking about yourself or the other person. The furry bodies on the end of the leash are easy to talk about. So read on. See if there is anything that might interest you and your dog. You both could use something new to do, couldn't you?

OBEDIENCE CLASSES

Even after you have successfully completed the training detailed in this book, you can still benefit from attending a good obedience class. Training in a class gives you the opportunity to train around the distractions of a room full of dogs and people. It provides your dog with exposure to a different place as well as socialization with dogs and strange people. A good instructor can help you learn how to read your dog. He or she can tell you when your dog is confused and when he is refusing to obey.

Finding a good class can be difficult. If you can't find a good one, don't go at all. Some classes are taught in such a violent manner that they can do damage to your dog and your relationship. Obedience classes are taught by all sorts of groups and individuals. It is important to know that dog trainers are not licensed in any way. Anyone can declare themselves a dog trainer, so you have to be very careful.

Classes can be offered by private individuals, privately owned training schools, boarding kennels, recreation departments, community colleges, kennel clubs, obedience clubs, or the adult education programs of your local school district. Any of these classes can be good or bad. The best classes are often not widely advertised because they are easily filled by word of mouth. Ask your friends who own dogs and your veterinarian for referrals.

In choosing an obedience class instructor, be sure not to equate dog training success with ability to instruct a class. These are related but different skills. A person may be able to train his dog to high honors in obedience competitions but be unable to teach someone else how to do it. Being able to teach people is different from being able to teach dogs, and both skills are needed to be a good dog obedience instructor. There is one national organization that does endorse obedience instructors. It is the National Association of Dog Obedience Instructors (NADOI). An instructor becomes a member of NADOI, which constitutes endorsement, by having at least a few years of experience teaching and by taking an extensive written test. Membership in NADOI at least indicates that an instructor is experienced and is interested enough in his profession to support such an organization. However, not all NADOI instructors may be to your liking, and there are many good obedience instructors that do not have NADOI endorsement.

Please don't take your dog to a kennel and leave him there to be trained. This type of training is often much more expensive but less successful. The trainer may be able to give you an impressive demonstration at the end of the training, but your dog is not going to continue living at the kennel, and the trainer won't be coming home with you to keep up the training. Even if you are given a lesson in how to handle your dog at the end of this type of training, one or two lessons is not enough to learn what to do if your dog does not respond to your commands. You will have missed the benefits of learning to read your dog as you train him as well as the benefits of the strong bond that develops between a dog and his trainer. Worse still, this kind of training can be abusive. You have no control over what is done to your dog in your absence.

Don't attend a class without finding out some information first. The best thing to do is to observe a class before you sign up. If an instructor or training organization won't let you do this, eliminate them from your list. What do you look for? First of all, do the dogs and owners look stressed, unhappy, or intimidated? Unless the dogs are shy, they should not be scared. Is the instructor clear in his instructions to the class? Remember, an obedience class instructor is teaching people, not training dogs. Does the instructor give the students a lot of positive reinforcement, pointing out when they do something well, or does he just yell when they do something wrong? He should be friendly and willing to talk to students before or after class. A sense of humor can be a real asset. Obedience classes do not need to be unpleasant to be effective. In fact, you will be more likely to complete the class if it is fun.

Observing a class prior to signing up is not always possible. If not, you have to ask a lot of questions. Here is a good list to go through:

1. Is the class size limited? I think eight to ten is an ideal number. If there are more, ask if there is an assistant instructor to help out. Obviously, the more people in a class, the less personal attention you will receive.

2. What is the instructor's experience? How did he learn to teach classes? Did he have some sort of apprenticeship? How long has he been teaching dog obedience classes? Of course, experience doesn't necessarily make someone good. In fact, someone who has taught for twenty years may be teaching by out-of-date methods. A good instructor tries to improve himself by reading books and dog training magazines and by attending training seminars.

3. Does the instructor use food rewards? If you agree with the ideas presented in this book, you may be uncomfortable with not using food and relying more on force. However, there are many different yet successful ways to train a dog. If the instructor doesn't allow the use of food in his class, make more effort to observe a class before signing up. Keep in mind that you can refuse to follow an instructor's directions if you feel something may be detrimental to your dog.

4. What is taught in the class? Does the instruction concentrate on practical training you can use every day, or is training for showing emphasized?

Of course, you will want to ask about the price and length of the class. An average class length is eight to twelve weeks, with the class meeting one hour per week. Are there homework sheets to help you with your practice at home? What equipment does the instructor prefer you to use? Does the instructor sound flexible in his training methods? Beware of any instructor who says there is only one way to train all dogs. Dogs and people are too different for one method to be effective for everyone.

Obedience classes are a good way to spend quality time with your dog. They will provide you with motivation to practice every week, if only because you won't want to look foolish at the next class. You and your dog will make new friends. If you find a good class, it can be lots of fun for both of you. Do it!

JOINING A DOG CLUB

A good way to get involved in activities with your dog, meet a wide variety of people, and further your knowledge about dogs is to join a dog club. Most clubs are affiliated with the American Kennel Club and are involved in holding shows and matches. There are at least a few in every state, but sometimes these clubs can be difficult to locate. Because they are nonprofit organizations run by volunteers, most cannot afford a listing in the phone book. The AKC can provide you with a list of the national clubs and the local clubs in your area. Their address is 51 Madison Avenue, New York, NY 10010; their phone number is (212) 696-8200. Not all dog clubs are affiliated with the AKC, however. Your veterinarian or the closest AKC club may be able to give you some information on these clubs.

Dog clubs vary in their character and their activities. AKC clubs can be all-breed clubs that may or may not include obedience training in their activities, or they may be obedience clubs. Clubs that are devoted to a single breed are called specialty clubs. Other AKC clubs have their main interest in hunting dogs. As with any organization some clubs are more welcoming to new members than others. All these clubs will be involved in putting on dog shows, matches, field trials, or hunting tests. In addition, they will probably have a variety of other activities. They may have monthly meetings that feature guest speakers or videotapes on dogs. They will probably have some social events, such as a Christmas party. Many AKC clubs hold handling or obedience classes. Some clubs give demonstrations at local shopping malls or county fairs, while others may sponsor seminars given by experts on some aspect of dogs.

A favorite activity of the club I belong to is visiting nursing homes with our dogs. There are clubs that specialize in this. We give a brief obedience demonstration, then do something fun, like playing musical chairs or square dancing with our dogs. After our program, we walk the dogs around to visit the residents, who pet the dogs and often share stories of a dog they have owned in the past. The activities directors of the nursing homes tell us that these are the most popular programs of the year. The dogs (and their owners!) love showing off. Everyone gets something out of it, not the least of which is our sense of self-satisfaction.

Whenever I have moved, one of the first things I do is contact the local dog club. It has always been a great way to make new friends. The diversity of people who belong to dog clubs is fascinating. Through dog clubs, my dogs have been able to participate in a variety of activities that provide them with the mental stimulation they need. Besides joining in club activities, I have always managed to find someone who shares my love for hiking with the dogs. The people I have met have greatly enriched my life. Maybe joining a dog club can do that for you, too!

DOG SHOWS

If you take pride in your dog's beauty, breeding, or in his training, you may want to try showing your dog. The competition at the dog shows is divided into two major divisions: breed (also called conformation) and obedience. The purpose of breed judging is to determine which dogs are the best examples of their breed and are therefore suitable for breeding. The dogs are judged on a combination of how well they measure up to a breed standard, which is a written

West Highland White Terriers being judged in breed (or conformation) competition.

description of what a particular breed should look like, and how well they move. This is why dogs are shown both standing still and trotting around the ring. Dogs are awarded the lifetime title of champion when they have accumulated fifteen points at various shows. The number of points awarded are based on the number of dogs entered. Spayed or neutered dogs may not be shown in breed competition.

The purpose of obedience competition, as stated in the AKC's obedience regulations, is "to demonstrate the usefulness of the pure-bred dog as a companion to man." In obedience competition, dogs are judged on performance only. Appearance does not count. There are three levels of competition: Novice, Open, and Utility. The titles awarded at each of the levels are Companion Dog (CD), Companion Dog Excellent (CDX), and Utility Dog (UD). Obedience titles are obtained by achieving a qualifying score in three shows at each level.

While I enjoy showing my dogs in breed, obedience competition is my real passion. Part of the reason is that obedience titles can be won without beating other people in competition. This means that there is a special camaraderie around the obedience rings. But the most important reason why I strive to put obedience titles on my dogs is that it provides a goal that stimulates me to perfect my communication with my dogs.

Dog shows are regulated by the American Kennel Club. This was the purpose for which the AKC was founded in 1884. Shortly thereafter, it took on the function of registering dogs. Obedience competition was not added until 1936. There are a few other much smaller organizations in the United States that also sponsor dog shows.

Dog shows are the most popular meeting ground of dog lovers. Some shows have more than three thousand entries. They provide an opportunity to learn more about dogs, make new friends, and travel. They also provide an opportunity to get up at ridiculous hours in the morning, drive many miles, spend hours outdoors in bad weather, and eat bad food, all in pursuit of a ribbon. It is a funny game, played with a dog for a partner.

Showing your dog can be an experience that is beneficial to your relationship with your dog, but it can also be detrimental. It is wonderful to travel with your dog to shows, sharing quality time together and the challenge of showing. On the other hand, the lust for wins and the ego gratification they bring can sometimes lead owners to neglect their dog's needs. The search for a winning show dog can result in an accumulation of dogs, whereby you can find yourself giving up the quality of human-dog relationship. It is important to keep in mind that dog shows satisfy people's needs, not dogs'.

HOW TO GET STARTED SHOWING YOUR DOG

The easiest way to get started showing your dog is to take a class to learn how to do it. There are two types of classes, one for each of the two types of showing: obedience classes and handling classes, which teach you how to show in breed.

While at first glance showing in the breed ring may not appear to be difficult, there is quite an art to doing it well. Just figuring out how the AKC point system works can be a challenge. Handling classes usually explain this, and teach you how to pose and gait your dog. These classes are harder to find than obedience classes. Some classes do not offer formal instruction, but just the chance to practice with your dog around other dogs. The best way to locate one is to call the AKC all-breed club closest to you. If you cannot find one, you might want to consider signing up for an obedience class instead. This is especially good if the person teaching the obedience class is familiar with the breed ring. Your dog would still get exposure to working around other dogs. Contrary to popular myth, you can show a dog in both breed and obedience. I do both with my dogs and feel the training in each complements the other.

To show your dog successfully in breed, you must develop a good understanding of the qualities being judged. To learn more about conformation and movement, you can read books or attend seminars. In addition, the AKC sells excellent videotapes interpreting the breed standard of many breeds as well as a videotape on canine structure and movement.

If you don't feel you can learn to handle your dog in the breed ring, there is another option. You can hire a professional handler to do it for you. A warning, however: hiring a handler is expensive. In fact, even if you handle your dog yourself, you can easily end up spending several thousand dollars in entry fees and travel expenses in order to put a championship title on your dog.

Before you invest much time and money in showing a dog in breed, it is a good idea to find out if your dog is of good enough quality to be competitive. Just because your dog is AKC registered does not mean it is show quality. Very few are. Your chances are best if one or both of your dog's parents have their championships. Try to have your dog evaluated by someone you trust who is knowledgeable about your breed. This could be someone who has finished a few championships on dogs of your breed, or it could be someone who handles dogs in the show ring professionally.

Professional handlers are rarely used in obedience, as most competitors handle and train their own dogs. Most people start with an obedience class. Look for a class taught by an instructor who has put a title, and preferably several titles, on dogs himself. The usual progression is to complete a beginner's class and then move up to a class that will start preparing you for competition.

Any AKC-registered dog that is not blind or deaf can compete in obedience, regardless of appearance. A dog can be spayed or neutered. Also, if you have a dog who appears to be pure-bred but is not AKC registered, you can apply to the AKC for an Indefinite Listing Privilege, which permits you to show that dog in obedience. As long as you are willing to put in the work involved, and your dog has no major temperament or physical problems, you should be able to earn an obedience title.

Before you walk into the obedience ring to show your dog, make sure you have obtained and read a copy of the obedience regulations. A single copy of this

The high jump is a part of advanced obedience competition.   (Border Collie)

is available at no charge by writing to the AKC (see "Joining a Dog Club" in this chapter for the AKC's address).

Joining a dog club is another good way to get started showing dogs. Members can share their knowledge with you. Also enjoying the company and support of club members at shows makes the show much more enjoyable.

If you cannot find classes, try reading some books on showing in either breed or obedience. A wealth of information is available by simply going to a show and watching. Once you feel you are ready to give it a try, the place to start is at a match.

Exercises Required to Obtain AKC Obedience Titles

Novice (CD)

1. Heel on leash and figure 8 . . . . Includes sitting at halt, about turns, changes of speed
2. Stand for examination . . . . Done off leash, with handler six feet away
3. Heel free and figure 8 . . . . Same pattern as heel on leash, but done off leash
4. Recall. . . . . Come when called from sit-stay thirty-five feet away
5. Long sit . . . . Done off leash for one minute with group of dogs
6. Long down. . . . . Done off leash for three minutes with group of dogs

Open (CDX)

1. Heel free and figure 8 . . . . Same as in Novice
2. Drop on recall. . . . . Dog must lie down on command while coming
3. Retrieve on flat . . . . A wooden or plastic dumbbell is retrieved
4. Retrieve over high jump. . . . . . Jump is 1¼ times the dog's height at the shoulder
5. Broad jump . . . . Jump's length is twice height of high jump
6. Long sit . . . . Done for three minutes with handler out of dog's sight
7. Long down. . . . . Done for five minutes with handler out of dog's sight

Utility (UD)

1. Signal exercise . . . . Heel, stand, down, sit, and come with hand signals only
2. Scent discrimination . . . . Dog finds handler's scent on one of ten metal and leather articles
3. Scent discrimination . . . . Same as above with another article
4. Directed retrieve . . . . Dog retrieves one of three gloves
5. Moving stand and exam. . . . . . Dog stays in stand while handler keeps moving
6. Directed jumping . . . . Dog goes away from handler, sits, and jumps as directed

MATCHES

Matches are practice dog shows. Their purpose is to give a person or dog new to the sport of dog showing an opportunity to practice before entering the big-time, licensed dog shows. Matches are smaller than regular dog shows, more informal, less expensive, and can usually be entered the same day instead of several weeks ahead of time, as is required for regular shows.

Just like big dog shows, matches usually offer both breed and obedience classes, but some of the classes are different. In breed, there are special classes for puppies, usually divided into 3-to-6-, 6-to-9-, and 9-to-12-month age groups. Offered in obedience at matches only is a class for beginner dogs called Pre-Novice. In this class, all the exercises are performed on leash. The exercises are heeling, including heeling in a figure 8 pattern; stand for exam; and recall with finish. Like Novice, there is a one-minute sit-stay and a three-minute down-stay done as a group.

Matches may or may not be AKC sanctioned. Those not AKC sanctioned are often called *fun matches*. In either case, the wins at a match do not count toward achieving a championship or an obedience title. Both are run according to AKC rules, except that mixed breeds are usually allowed to compete in fun matches, and you are allowed to correct your dog for mistakes in obedience, which is not allowed at sanctioned matches.

Matches also provide a training ground for judges. Keep this in mind when you enter one. Your dog may be scored differently in obedience or placed differently in breed by a more experienced judge at a regular show.

CANINE GOOD CITIZEN TEST

As a means of fighting the growing antidog sentiment in the country, the AKC introduced the Canine Good Citizen program in 1989. It is open to mixed breeds as well as pure-bred dogs. The purpose of the test is to demonstrate that a dog has good manners. It is noncompetitive. A certificate will be given to all dogs that pass. This is not considered an AKC title, which means that it will not be registered as part of a dog's record at the AKC as other titles are, such as obedience titles and breed championships.

A dog must pass all ten parts of the test to earn a certificate. All parts are performed on leash. The ten parts are:

1. Appearance and grooming. Owner must present proof of vaccinations. Evaluator will brush the dog.
2. Accepting a stranger. Evaluator and owner will shake hands.
3. Walk on loose lead. Dog will heel and execute turns and halts.
4. Walking through a crowd. Dog should walk without straining at leash, passing close to several people.
5. Sit for exam. Evaluator will approach and pet dog.

The A-frame obstacle is part of most agility trials. (Dalmatian)

6. Sit and down on command. Owner may use more than one command but not force dog into position.
7. Stay in sit or down. Owner will drop leash, walk twenty feet away, and return.
8. Reaction to another dog. Two handlers and dogs approach each other, stop and shake hands.
9. Reaction to distractions. Distractions may be a jogger passing by, a bicycle, a shopping cart, people acting excited, or a sudden noise.
10. Dog left alone. Dog will be fastened with leash while owner goes out of sight for five minutes.

This program is just getting off the ground as this book is being written. It is hard to say now how popular it will become.

AGILITY

Agility is an exciting new dog sport recently imported to the United States from England. It is best described as an obstacle course for dogs. The sport originated in the early 1970s as a police dog competition designed to appeal to spectators. Its rapid growth in the United States is evidence of its appeal to dogs, trainers, and spectators alike.

Agility courses generally consist of about fourteen obstacles. Included in these obstacles are tunnels, a raised "dog walk," hurdles, poles to weave in and out of, hoops to jump through, and a seesaw. Dogs run the course individually, against a clock. They are off leash, with their handlers running beside them. The height of the obstacles varies with the height of the dog, so toy dogs can participate as well as large dogs.

At the time this book is being written, the sport lacks a single national organization, so there are different sets of rules used. Agility clubs are springing up around the country to enjoy and promote the sport. Many established dog clubs are adding agility to their activities. The American Kennel Club has expressed interest in making agility one of its own programs and allows agility demonstrations to be held at dog shows.

If you have an opportunity to try agility, don't pass it up. Your dog doesn't have to have much training. The initial training is done on leash. It helps if your dog has had some prior exposure to jumping. Even dogs who are a little frightened at first gain confidence from the experience. The dogs are so pleased with themselves when they master a new obstacle. Your dog will love it!

SPECIAL ACTIVITIES FOR SPECIAL BREEDS

Lure coursing, herding tests, Schutzhund, and AKC hunting tests are all examples of dog sports that are based on the job for which breeds were developed. Man's competitive nature led to the design of ways to test these skills. Such tests are also a means to identify and measure these instinctive behaviors so

These Borzoi are being released at the start of a lure course.

This Belgian Tervuren is learning to herd sheep.

they can be preserved in breeding programs, since most dogs no longer have the opportunity to engage in the work for which they were bred. Other similar dog sports not described here are terrier trials and sled-dog racing.

Because these dog sports utilize the instincts of the dogs, the dogs love them. They are a fun and challenging way for you and your dog to spend time together. If you own one of the breeds used in these sports, try to go see such an event. Like dog showing, if kept in the proper prospective, they provide a fascinating hobby and an opportunity to make new friends. Giving your dog the opportunity to make use of his instinctive behavior will make him happier, and it is a great way to continue building your relationship with your dog.

Lure Coursing

Lure coursing is a modern version of a sport that has been practiced since ancient times. Coursing on live game is illegal in most places, so an artificial lure is now used. This is done by dragging a white plastic bag at fast speeds along the ground in a pattern full of irregular turns in an open field. The breeds allowed to compete are Afghans, Basenjis, Borzois, Greyhounds, Ibizen Hounds, Irish Wolfhounds, Pharaoh Hounds, Salukis, Scottish Deerhounds, and Whippets. This group of breeds are called sight hounds, because they hunt by sight.

Lure coursing relies on the dog's instinct to chase a moving object, and little training is required, other than making sure a dog is in adequate physical condition. Usually three dogs run at a time. It is beautiful and inspiring to watch. Most sight hounds love it, and it gives them an opportunity to exercise. As mentioned above, lure coursing also enables breeders to evaluate their stock to chose suitable animals for breeding. Practice runs are often available for a small cost after licensed trials.

Lure coursing is not judged on speed alone. Rather the dogs receive scores for agility, following the lure, enthusiasm, endurance, and speed. Winners receive ribbons. Points are awarded based on how many dogs are beaten at each course, with one hundred points being required to attain a field championship.

Note that this is different from Greyhound racing. First of all, it is open to more breeds. The courses are not run on a track, but in an open field. The dogs involved in lure coursing are people's pets, not part of a racing industry. There is no gambling involved in this sport.

Lure coursing is not currently regulated by the American Kennel Club, but it may be in the future. The organization that currently regulates the sport is the American Sighthound Field Association (ASFA). You can find out more about lure coursing by contacting the ASFA. The current address is often published in popular dog magazines.

Herding Tests

Herding is an aspect of canine hunting behavior that man has made good use of. Various hunting behaviors present in our dogs' wolflike ancestors were selectively bred over many generations to produce dogs exhibiting special abilities, such as sight hounds and herding dogs.

In 1989 the American Kennel Club introduced a set of herding tests open to all AKC-registered herding breeds. These breeds include the Belgian Shepherd breeds, Collies, Corgis, German Shepherds, and Shetland Sheepdogs. There are two types of tests: the Herding Instinct Tests, which are noncompetitive and require less training; and the Herding Trials, which are competitive. Herding Trials offer three titles based on increasingly difficult tests, as well as a herding champion title based on wins and points from the most advanced test.

In the AKC program, the Preliminary Test is an instinct test that requires no training or experience on the part of the dog or the dog's owner. The livestock used can be sheep, ducks, or cattle. To receive a qualifying score in this test, your dog must show sustained interest in the livestock either by circling them or by following them. Dogs are tested off leash or with the leash dragging. Dogs that show no interest, are too aggressive, or are afraid of the livestock will not pass.

Schutzhund

The Schutzhund sport originated in Germany in the early 1900s as a means of testing whether German Shepherds had the qualities necessary for breeding. It is still used for this purpose in Germany today, and is a growing sport in the United States. Any breed may participate, although the jump requirements eliminate small dogs. The breeds used most often in this sport are German Shepherds, Rottweilers, Dobermans, Belgian Sheepdogs, and Bouviers des Flandres. Some organizations allow mixed breeds to compete.

A Schutzhund test involves three parts: tracking, obedience, and protection. All three parts are tested in one day. The titles that can be obtained are Schutzhund I, II, and III. A passing score is required in each of the three parts to get a title. The tracking portion of Schutzhund I involves a track laid by the handler that is 350 paces long and at least twenty minutes old. Two articles that the dog must find are dropped along the track.

In the obedience portion, the exercises are not easy, even at the first level of Schutzhund I. They include heeling on and off leash, sit while the handler keeps moving, recall from a down position, retrieve, retrieve over a 39½-inch (1 meter) jump, sending the dog away from you about twenty-five paces, and a down-stay.

Although the protection phase of the Schutzhund sport is assigned the same number of points as the obedience and tracking phases, the protection work is the identifying characteristic of Schutzhund. To achieve the Schutzhund I title, a dog is required to search out the hidden villain, also called the agitator or decoy, and bark at him when he finds him. The dog should not bite the agitator as long as he stands still. In the next part, the agitator charges out of a hiding place as if to attack the handler. The dog should attack without a command and bite the agitator on the arm. When the agitator stands still, the dog should stop biting on command. The final part is the courage test. In this test, the dog is sent to chase

This German Shepherd is learning protection work in preparation for a Schutzhund trial.

Giving the direction for a retrieve is part of the AKC retriever hunting test. (Golden Retriever)

the agitator, who is running away. Then the agitator will turn and charge at the dog, waving a stick. The dog should not hesitate to attack. Again, the dog should stop attacking on command. The handler and dog escort the agitator off the field, with the dog remaining at heel.

There is more than one Schutzhund organization in the United States, including the United Schutzhund Clubs of America (USCA) and the North American Schutzhund Association (NASA), each with slightly different rules. Joining a Schutzhund club is the best way to pursue such training.

A Schutzhund-trained dog is not an attack dog. He should be friendly and approachable by anyone who is not hostile and he should make a good family pet. Because of the aggression being taught, such training should not be undertaken lightly. An owner must be very sure of his control over his dog.

AKC Hunting Tests

Do you want to see if your Golden Retriever, Irish Setter, or Springer Spaniel still has the hunting instincts for which his breed was developed? Then the AKC's hunting tests are for you. Hunting tests got their start when the first test was held in 1985 as a noncompetitive alternative to field trails. Field trials are expensive and time consuming, certainly beyond the reach of the average dog owner. For instance, pointing breed field trials require that the dogs be handled from horseback. In contrast, handlers walk in the hunting tests for the same breeds.

The hunting tests are divided into tests for retrievers, pointers, and spaniels. There are three levels of difficulty. After qualifying a specified number of times, your dog is awarded the titles of junior hunter, senior hunter, or the most difficult, master hunter.

As an example, let's look at the requirements for the junior hunter retriever test. The retriever must do a minimum of four retrieves, two on land and two on water. Distances should not exceed one hundred yards. The dog must retrieve to hand, not dropping the bird or refusing to give it up. Live ducks are used and shot. Dogs are scored on marking (memory of where the bird has fallen), style, nose (scenting ability), perseverance, and trainability. The tests should imitate natural hunting conditions as much as possible.

These tests are rapidly increasing in popularity. If you want to see one, contact the AKC for help in finding the one nearest you.

FUN AND FITNESS WITH YOUR DOG

Most dogs love to be outdoors and active. Finding ways to indulge your dog in these pleasures may introduce you to new activities and new ways of enjoying old ones.

What do you do if you live in Vermont, where snow covers the ground for many months, and you have to exercise two big dogs? When I was in that position, I learned to cross-country ski, which proved to be great exercise for me

Cross-country skiing is a good way to enjoy the snow with your dog. (Belgian Tervuren)

Many dogs love to go swimming. (Golden Retriever)

and my dogs. The dogs had to learn to stay out of the way of swinging ski poles, heel with a skier, and get off the trail when snowmobiles approached. Mine had to learn that when I fell, it was not an invitation to play. One of the hardest things to teach them, and something that was the cause of a few spectacular crashes until they learned, was that when they were running in front of us on a downhill section and we yelled their names, we did *not* want them to stop and turn around to look at us!

In the summer, when it is too hot for your dog to exercise any other way, swimming is the activity of choice. You will probably have to get into the water with him to build his confidence about stepping off into water that is over his head. Support him under his belly while he gets the feel of it. Don't count on your dog being able to swim instinctively. I have seen dogs jump into the water and let themselves sink without making any effort to save themselves. Dogs may also flail around with their front legs and try to climb out of the water, spinning in circles and going nowhere. It helps if your dog can play with another dog who loves to swim. If he likes to retrieve, you might be able to entice him into swimming by throwing something just a little farther each time until he is forced to swim. You can introduce puppies as young as eight weeks old to the water. It takes a little longer for an adult dog to relax in the water, but most can learn to love it. Swimming is the perfect exercise for older dogs with arthritis.

Hiking is a great activity to share with a dog. This may take the form of a two-hour walk in the woods, or an overnight expedition. I live along the Appalachian Trail, and I meet dogs who are hiking with their owners all the way from Georgia to Maine. A good combination is hiking with a dog play group. It is so relaxing to walk and talk with good friends, while the dogs play with each other.

There are other ways to share the outdoors with your dog. We've already discussed jogging with your dog in the chapter on exercising your dog. You could take your dog with you on horseback rides or let him gather all the tennis balls you hit over the fence. We enjoy canoeing with our dogs. Believe it or not, they quickly learn to balance. A good response to the "stay" command is a necessity when they want to jump out to chase a duck! Whatever you do, dogs (*trained* dogs, that is) and the outdoors are a natural combination.

TO BREED OR NOT TO BREED

When talking about things to do with your dog, breeding your dog is something that might come to mind. Bringing new lives into the world is a responsibility that should not be taken lightly, especially in a world where millions of unwanted dogs are killed every year.

There are different kinds of breeders. Good breeders strive to breed the healthiest, most beautiful dogs with the best temperaments possible. They show their dogs to get an objective opinion about the quality of their dogs. They are knowledgeable about the genetic diseases of their breed and have had their dogs tested to reduce the possibility of passing these genes on. These puppies come with a health and temperament guarantee.

Good breeders are also very selective about the homes in which they place their puppies. They will interview prospective buyers extensively. If they cannot find the right homes, they are prepared to keep the puppies until they do. They put great effort into educating their puppy buyers about how to raise and care for their dog. If for any reason you cannot keep your dog, good breeders want to know about it, because they feel responsible for each and every puppy they have produced. If there is any way they can, they will take the dog back, at any age. Their passion for their breed is evident when you speak to them.

There are also what is commonly referred to as "backyard" breeders. These are people with no real knowledge of the breed. They just think their dog is nice and that it would be fun to have puppies. Besides, they might be able to make some money. After all, they paid enough for their dog. These casual breeders' choice of stud is based on convenience rather than quality; they use any dog of the same breed who happens to live close by. They have probably heard of hip dysplasia but don't really know what it is. Their dog seems fine, so they are not worried about the disease. They don't know that their dog is too young to show any signs of the hereditary disease unless she was x-rayed. Their knowledge of how to housebreak and train a puppy is limited, so they won't be able to give you any advice. This kind of breeder doesn't really care anyway. That's the buyer's problem. As long as you have the money, the puppy is yours.

What kind of breeder would you rather buy a puppy from? What kind of breeder do you want to be? If you can't be a good breeder, you shouldn't be a breeder at all.

If you want to be a good breeder, the first question you should ask yourself is whether your dog is of good enough quality to breed. Just because your dog is a nice family pet with AKC papers is not reason enough. Because there are a limited number of good homes available, only the best dogs should be bred. Your dog should have a perfect temperament, be a good specimen of his or her breed, and be free of all hereditary diseases. Hereditary diseases are abundant in pure-bred dogs. Just because your dog seems healthy does not mean he or she doesn't have such diseases as hip dysplasia or cataracts. *You don't know if you haven't had him or her checked.* It is irresponsible to breed a dog without a thorough check for all hereditary diseases known to occur in the breed.

Be honest with yourself in assessing your dog's temperament. Don't make excuses for your dog's shy or aggressive personality. There is no way to know for certain if the problem is hereditary or not, so don't take the chance of breeding more puppies with a similar problem. Also consider your dog's trainability in evaluating his or her temperament.

The second thing you should ask yourself is if you have the qualities and knowledge necessary to be a good breeder. Do you know the signs that your dog is having difficulty delivering a puppy and is in need of immediate veterinary attention? Do you know what to do if a puppy doesn't start breathing when delivered? Do you know how to choose a stud? Do you know what your state laws are regarding the sale of puppies?

Do you have the time? There are several things that can cause a mother dog

If your life is already hectic, do you really have the time to raise a litter of puppies?

to be unable to nurse her puppies, such as a cesarean delivery or mastitis (an infection of the breasts). In such cases, you will need to feed the puppies often and around the clock. Even after they are weaned, you will have to be there four times a day to feed them. You will also spend a lot of time cleaning up after them. If your life is already hectic, do you really have the time?

Then there is the problem of placing the puppies. Do you feel you can adequately screen buyers to prevent your puppy from being placed in a home where he will not be properly cared for? For instance, what are your feelings about placing a puppy in a home without a fenced yard? Are you sure there is a demand for puppies of your breed? If your breed is popular, there may not only be a demand for puppies, but there may also be a flood of them advertised in the newspaper. What are you going to do if you cannot find homes for the puppies?

You can be responsible for a tremendous amount of dog suffering if you do not carefully interview and screen your buyers. An all-too-common story is a puppy that is left alone all day without being confined while his owners work. When the owners return home to find their furniture ripped to shreds and messes all over the floor, they beat the dog and chain him up in the backyard. The dog suffers at the end of the chain, receiving inadequate care and no love, until he is abandoned at the local animal shelter and mercifully euthanized. Don't kid yourself. This happens to pure-bred dogs as well as to mixed breeds.

Think about the millions of unwanted dogs that are killed annually. Is it really necessary for you to breed your dog?

CONCLUSION

All the activities mentioned here are growing in popularity. They are actually just a sampling of the many activities available to dog owners. Flyball, field trials, scent hurdle racing, terrier go-to-grounds, and cart pulling are just a few of many more. Many of these activities are new. All this reflects the growing interest people have in doing things with their dogs. The AKC has responded to these new demands by recently adding several activities that evaluate how dogs perform, rather than just how they look. These changes also reflect a growing appreciation for a dog's intelligence and respect for his abilities.

If you aren't interested in pursuing any of these activities with your dog, please remember his need for mental stimulation. Include him in family activities as much as possible. Take him places with you, on errands or to the kids' soccer games. Try taking your dog with you when you travel. The inconveniences involved will be compensated for by the interesting experiences you will have.

What you get out of your relationship with your dog is proportional to what you put into it. Anything you do to spend quality time with your dog will improve your relationship, but facing new challenges and learning together will give your relationship a unique depth. The rewards are worth it.

11

Lessons to Learn from Our Dogs

THERE ARE LESSONS you can learn from your dog and the process of training him that have wider application than just to dog training. What you have learned in training your dog can be applied in your relationships with humans. Developing a good relationship, be it with a dog or with another person, involves similar skills.

Dogs offer good examples for us. Everyone who owns a dog knows how pleasing it is to be greeted by their dog when they return home. Their dog doesn't complain about what happened to him during the day, he isn't mad about a fight from the night before, and he doesn't make any immediate demands. He is just happy to see you. Wouldn't you like to be greeted that way by everyone? Try it yourself. Greet someone, like your husband or wife when he or she gets home from work, or your kids when they get home from school, the same way as your dog greets you. No, I don't mean wagging your tail or jumping up on them. I mean meet them at the door with a smile, acting happy to see them, and listen, refraining from complaints or demands.

By learning from our dogs about building a good relationship and the power of positive reinforcement, about the importance of nonverbal communication and who we are, and most of all about love, we may finally become as noble as our dogs think we are.

Dogs make good listeners. (Golden Retriever)

BUILDING A GOOD RELATIONSHIP

Patience, good listening skills, empathy, tolerance, realistic expectations—these are all skills that make for a good relationship, whether it be with a dog or a person.

In the first chapter and throughout this book realistic expectations regarding your dog have been emphasized. Whenever your expectations of your dog are not fulfilled, your disappointment and frustration can lead you to dislike your dog. The same is true of human relationships. When a person doesn't live up to someone else's expectations, serious problems develop in the relationship. False expectations can lead you to think that the person or dog is purposely acting in a way to hurt you. The relationship then becomes one of adversaries. The adversarial relationship people develop with their dogs reminds me of the adversarial relationships people have with each other. It may be between marriage partners, between parent and child, or with anybody. Fighting develops. Dogs are punished; people hurt each other. It is impossible to build a good relationship without realistic expectations.

Tolerance is based on realistic expectations. You have to develop a lot of tolerance to live with a dog. He has different needs and priorities. For example, keeping your house clean is not as important to your dog as it is to you. When you own a dog, you have to learn to tolerate having dirt tracked in and hair shedding. Your dog has shown you that in order for him to meet your need for a well-behaved dog, you have to meet his need for exercise. This understanding of needs and priorities is essential for good human relationships, too.

Wrong assumptions regarding the meaning of another's behavior are destructive to good relationships. When you return home to find that your dog has destroyed something in your absence, it is tempting to think that he has done this out of spite. As was discussed in Chapter 8, this isn't true; usually destructive chewing is done out of fear of being left alone. Assuming your dog chewed on the woodwork because he resents being left alone is a reflection of feeling guilty about leaving a dog alone. These wrong assumptions can lead to harming your relationship with your dog by inappropriate punishment.

The same thing can happen with wrong assumptions in human relationships. Take for example a child who is caught stealing. The parents assume that the child is simply greedy and wants more than he has. The child is punished. However, the real reason for the stealing may have been that the child craves the parents' attention and thinks this is the only way of getting it. The solution to the real problem is more than punishment.

Good communication is the foundation of all good relationships, and listening is the foundation of good communication. Most people talk to their dogs, not because their dogs can understand them, and not because they think their dog is going to offer good advice, but because dogs are such good listeners. They can't talk back, they can't interrupt you, and they can't argue with you. They give you their full attention.

Mutual good listening is true of good dog training and good friendships.

You have to "listen" to your dog's body language to train him well. You also have to train him to listen to you. I am fascinated by the similarities between the techniques used to train dogs for obedience competition to ensure they aren't distracted in the ring while performing and the listening skills taught in marriage improvement seminars. All your relationships would be better if you learned to listen as well as your dog does.

Many people find it easier to develop a good relationship with a dog than with another person. Dogs can't talk back and aren't as judgmental. Training your dog can give you the insight necessary to apply these skills to other areas of your life.

THE POWER OF POSITIVE REINFORCEMENT

The most important lesson you can learn from training your dog with the techniques described in this book is the power of positive reinforcement. People respond to positive reinforcement just as well as dogs do.

One reason my obedience classes are successful is because I pay special attention to positively reinforcing the owners. I don't use food, of course; praise is a good reward for people. In a class of beginners, it would be easy to constantly find fault with their performance and only point out what they are doing wrong, but that would be discouraging and would lead to people dropping out of the class. Rather, I make a point of praising the owners. Even with the worst-behaved dog in class I manage to find some small improvement to praise. The owners feel good about their accomplishments, so they keep practicing, in spite of the many frustrations involved in training. The owners are eventually rewarded with a trained dog.

You can integrate positive reinforcement into many aspects of your life. When my husband wanted to increase the number of patients he saw in a day, he pushed his staff to speed up and become more efficient. It didn't work. Then I suggested trying positive reinforcement. He offered a bonus if a certain goal was met. This time productivity increased, and everyone was happier. Making positive reinforcement part of your life is as simple as putting more energy in saying thank you and rewarding people when they do something you like, and less in complaining when they do something wrong.

All the disadvantages of punishing a dog apply to humans, too. Just as in dogs, punishment can create fear, avoidance, resentment, and secretiveness. It cuts off communication, and it doesn't teach what you want. Look how ineffective prison is as a punishment for criminals.

Punishment is as destructive to human relationships as it is to dogs. A common reaction of a wife to a husband who frequently comes home late from work is to criticize him and start a fight; she is punishing him. The husband, dreading the scene when he comes home from work, avoids the situation by coming home later and later. A better tactic for the wife would be to ignore the late arrivals and reward him when he comes home on time. At first, he may even have to be rewarded for coming home a little less late. The reward could be meeting him at the door in a good mood, listening sympathetically to his complaints about work, and getting him something to drink. He may be more anxious to come home on time in the future. While punishment works in some situations, it must be balanced by positive reinforcement to maintain a good relationship.

It is hard to break the habit of punishment. It is the method most people choose to deal with problem behavior, whether it is a person or a dog who is misbehaving. I often have trouble convincing people to stop punishing their dogs, even though they admit that the punishment is not working. Punishment is part of our culture. It provides a release for anger and a means to dominate and control. The world would be a better place if the urge to punish and control was replaced by the urge to understand and help.

THE IMPORTANCE OF NONVERBAL COMMUNICATION

Dogs always seem so honest and sensitive—qualities we would like to have in ourselves and in the people around us. That dogs have these qualities is related to the fact that they communicate nonverbally. They seem honest because, without being able to talk, they cannot lie.

Dogs seem sensitive because they read our body language. They are good at it because this is the way they communicate with each other. Dogs cannot be misled by the things we say. We cannot hide our feelings from them with words. For instance, when someone asks you how you are, you may respond by saying you are fine, even when you are not. The person to whom you are speaking may miss the nonverbal messages that say you are not fine, such as slumped body posture and a depressed tone of voice if you are sad, or tense body posture and an abrupt tone of voice if you are angry. Your dog would never make this mistake, and neither should you when you are communicating with other people or you will miss an important part of their message. If you ask someone what's wrong, and they reply "Nothing," but their body language says something else, don't ignore the real message. Reading and responding to body language improve communication; this, in turn, improves relationships.

DOGS ARE OUR MIRRORS

Often the first awareness I have of being in a particular mood is when it is reflected in my dog. Her behavior reflects my tension or my relaxation, my anxiety or my peacefulness, my depression or my happiness. When I am in a bad mood, I often find her hiding in her crate, avoiding me. Seeing this makes me feel terrible. I can then put things in perspective and relax, much to the relief of the rest of my family. My dog, acting as a mirror, has helped me to see myself.

Dogs act as mirrors in many ways. Our choice of dogs tells us something about ourselves. Why is it that some people choose to rescue dogs from Humane

Dogs mirror our personalities.

Societies, while others choose to buy expensive, pure-bred dogs? And what about your choice of breed? My choice of a Russian Wolfhound and a Greyhound as pets reflects my desire to project to the world an image of elegance and sophistication. My husband, on the other hand, chose a Belgian Tervuren, a breed that is not readily recognized and in fact is often mistaken for a Collie-Shepherd mix. This reflects his distaste for displays of wealth. Both of our choices of unusual breeds reveal a mutual desire to be seen as a little different from other people.

A dog's sensitivity makes him a wonderful mirror of your moods. The way you have raised and trained him also reveals something about yourself. Training your dog magnifies the mirror effect, because your relationship is intensified by the communication effort. Are you apt to lose your temper with your dog, or are you quick to blame him when he doesn't understand what you want? When you become frustrated, do you give up, or do you tend to resort to physical force? Are you afraid that if you are assertive in your training efforts your dog will not love you? What does the way you train your dog tell you about yourself?

As an obedience instructor, I see many examples of the mirror effect. For instance, there is always a strong correlation between well-behaved dogs and well-behaved children. The dog who cannot concentrate and is easily distracted is a clear reflection of his owner, who arrives late to class, has forgotten her dog's training collar, and misses half the instructions because she is talking to someone else. The easygoing dog has an equally laid-back owner. A nervous dog mirrors tension within the family.

Our dogs exhibit the effects of stress. They reflect erratic, hectic lifestyles and stressful environments in their behavior and with physical problems. Like their human owners, dogs can develop intestinal problems or nervous behaviors. Signs of stress in your dog are warning signals that you should heed for your own health, as well as your dog's. A simple thing like a long walk may alleviate stress for both of you.

This ability of dogs to act as mirrors is clearly seen in the story of Lisa, a teenage girl, and her German Shepherd, Mandi. Mandi was three years old and not housebroken, even though she had always lived indoors. As I talked with Lisa about this, she told me of the inconsistent and confusing attempts of her parents to housebreak the dog. Her father's idea of housebreaking was to hit Mandi when she relieved herself in the house. Lisa's mother felt sorry for the rough treatment Mandi received from her husband and tried to compensate by adopting a permissive attitude toward Mandi's accidents. To complicate the matter further, Lisa's mother had told her husband she didn't want him to hit the dog, so he only punished Mandi when his wife was not around.

Lisa realized that Mandi's housebreaking training was a reflection of her own upbringing. As a result of this inconsistent and confusing treatment, Mandi and Lisa had similar personalities; they were both timid, passive, and insecure. Using her dog as a mirror, Lisa was able to understand herself.

When Lisa's mother died, Lisa came to live with my husband and me. Mandi was placed in a loving home. She is now happy and housebroken. Lisa is a beautiful, confident young woman who now has her Animal Health Technician degree and received an award when she graduated for being the best all-around student in both academic and extracurricular activities. Positive reinforcement, consistency, and unconditional love worked wonders for both of them.

UNCONDITIONAL LOVE

The greatest lesson dogs can teach us is unconditional love. This admirable trait was memorialized in a well-known speech given in 1869 as part of a closing argument in a court case involving the death of a dog.

> The one absolutely unselfish friend that a man can have in this selfish world, the one that never deserts him and the one that never proves ungrateful or treacherous is his dog. . . . He will kiss the hand that has no food to offer, he will lick the wounds and sores that come in encounters with the roughness of the world. He guards the sleep of his pauper master as if he were a prince. When all other friends desert he remains. When riches take wings and reputation falls to pieces, he is as constant in his love as the sun in its journey through the heavens. . . .

People's craving for such love is undoubtedly why dog ownership is so popular. Dogs don't judge us. They don't care what we look like or how much money we make. They don't care if we say or do something stupid. The unconditional nature of their love is the reason dogs are such good therapists in nursing homes and with mentally disturbed people.

The example of unconditional love given to us by our dogs should be followed by us in our relationships with other humans. It is the kind of love that makes us feel that someone will love us no matter what we say or do. They may not like our actions, but they will always love us. It is love without conditions attached to it. Conditional love is the feeling that someone will stop loving you if you do not perform correctly or if you do not act as expected, such as a belief that your parents will stop loving you if you do not get good grades in school or that your husband will leave you if you argue with him.

We can provide others with the same sense of security, acceptance, and love that our dogs give us by giving them unconditional love. Children need it to grow into mentally healthy adults; marriages need it to be happy. It is the greatest gift your dog gives you; it is the best gift you can give to another.

LOVE TO GROW ON

Falling in love with a puppy is like falling in love with a human. It is the exciting beginning of a relationship, but it is only a temporary state. Reality soon sets in. With a puppy, reality is accidents on the rug, chewed shoes, and not coming when called. With a human, it is irritating habits and different priorities.

For the relationship to continue, whether it be with a dog or another

As the training goes, the love grows.

person, this temporary love has to grow into real love. If it doesn't, the relationship ends. In humans, this often means a divorce. Unfortunately, dogs pay a higher price when the love fails to grow. They are isolated in a cage in the backyard or abandoned at the local animal shelter to face probable death.

Real love is the act of extending yourself to help another achieve happiness. For it to develop there has to be a commitment beyond keeping a dog or spouse as long as they make you happy. Realistic expectations, good communication, sensitivity, understanding, and unconditional love are all ingredients that contribute to its growth.

Training a dog should be an expression of real love. It should develop mutual communication and respect. It should not be done purely to meet your own needs, nor should it be done to dominate. Training is giving up something of yourself, your time and energy, to meet your dog's need for mental and physical exercise. It is striking the right balance between the necessity of exercising control for your dog's well-being and allowing him freedom to be a dog. As the training goes, the love grows. And so will you.